Leading School Culture through Teacher Voice and Agency

Leading School Culture through Teacher Voice and Agency helps school leaders uncover, understand, and build the skill set to engage teachers in the work of school culture as they navigate the changes needed to improve the achievement for all students. This book presents a Framework for School Culture that explores how school culture, when acted upon through teacher voice and agency, is an untapped resource that can move schools forward. By supporting teacher voice and agency, the school and its teachers and leaders move toward taking collective responsibility for sustaining a culture of improvement that is stronger and more responsive.

This research-grounded book is rich in practical tools to help leaders work with teachers, ensuring all the educators in a school are taking ownership over their own learning and developing the skills to reshape school culture to ensure students, teachers, and community members thrive.

Sally J. Zepeda is Professor of Educational Administration and Policy at the University of Georgia, USA.

Philip D. Lanoue is an Educational Consultant and the 2015 American Association of School Administrators (AASA) National Superintendent of the Year, USA.

Grant M. Rivera is Superintendent of Marietta City Schools, Georgia, USA.

David R. Shafer is Chief Entrepreneur with Cognia, Inc., and he serves as School Board Director with the Spring-Ford Area School District, Pennsylvania, USA.

Also Available from Sally J. Zepeda and Philip D. Lanoue

Professional Development: What Works (3rd Edition)
Sally J. Zepeda

**The Leader's Guide to Working with Underperforming Teachers:
Overcoming Marginal Teaching and Getting Results**
Sally J. Zepeda

**Job-embedded Professional Development:
Support, Collaboration, and Learning in Schools**
Sally J. Zepeda

**Informal Classroom Observations on the Go:
Feedback, Discussion, and Reflection (3rd Edition)**
Sally J. Zepeda

**The Principal as Instructional Leader:
A Handbook for Supervisors (3rd Edition)**
Sally J. Zepeda

**Instructional Supervision:
Applying Tools and Concepts (4th Edition)**
Sally J. Zepeda

Supervision Across the Content Areas
Sally J. Zepeda and R. Stewart Mayers

Instructional Leadership for School Improvement
Sally J. Zepeda

**Developing the Organizational Culture of the Central Office:
Collaboration, Connectivity, and Coherence**
Sally J. Zepeda, Mary Lynne Derrington, and Philip D. Lanoue

**A Leadership Guide to Navigating the Unknown in Education:
New Narratives amid COVID-19**
Sally J. Zepeda and Philip D. Lanoue

Leading School Culture through Teacher Voice and Agency

Sally J. Zepeda, Philip D. Lanoue, Grant M. Rivera, and David R. Shafer

Routledge
Taylor & Francis Group

NEW YORK AND LONDON

Cover image: © Getty Images

First published 2023
by Routledge
605 Third Avenue, New York, NY 10158

and by Routledge
4 Park Square, Milton Park, Abingdon, Oxon, OX14 4RN

Routledge is an imprint of the Taylor & Francis Group, an informa business

Library of Congress Cataloging-in-Publication Data
A catalog record for this book has been requested

ISBN: 978-1-032-11164-3 (hbk)
ISBN: 978-1-032-12020-1 (pbk)
ISBN: 978-1-003-22265-1 (ebk)

DOI: 10.4324/9781003222651

Typeset in Optima
by Apex CoVantage, LLC

Contents

About the Authors

Sally J. Zepeda, Ph.D. is Professor in Educational Administration and Policy at the University of Georgia where she teaches courses and conducts research related to instructional supervision, professional development, and teacher evaluation. Before entering higher education, Dr. Zepeda served as a high school English teacher, assistant principal, and principal. From these experiences, she is considered a bridge-builder bringing light on the intersections between practice and research.

Dr. Zepeda has worked with many school systems in the United States and overseas, especially the Middle East, to support teacher and leader development. Nationally and internationally, she has designed teacher and leader evaluation systems, instructional coaching programs, model system-wide strategic plans as well as degree and academic programs.

Philip D. Lanoue, Ph.D. has a demonstrated record in leading school trans-formation at the building and district levels. Dr. Lanoue is the 2015 American Association of School Administrators (AASA) National Superintendent of the Year, as well as the 2015 Georgia Superintendent of the Year. Before serving at the superintendent level across two systems, Dr. Lanoue was a high school principal, and he was named Principal of the Year by the Vermont National Association of School Principals.

Dr. Lanoue served on the White House Policy Advisory for the New Generation High School Summit and the ConnectED Future Ready White House Summit. Dr. Lanoue co-authored *The Emerging Work of Today's Superintendent: Leading Schools and Communities to Educate All Children* with Dr. Sally J. Zepeda (Rowman & Littlefield and jointly published by the American Association of

School Administrators); *Developing the Organizational Culture of the Central Office: Collaboration, Connectivity, and Coherence* with Dr. Sally J. Zepeda (Routledge); and *A Leadership Guide to Navigating the Unknown in Education: New Narratives amid COVID-19* with Dr. Sally J. Zepeda (Routledge).

Grant M. Rivera, Ed.D. believes great schools are built on the combined strength of supported families, talented educators, and an engaged community. Prior to his current position as superintendent of Marietta City Schools, Dr. Rivera served as Chief of Staff and principal of two high schools in the Cobb County School District, the second largest district in Georgia. He is nationally recognized for innovative work that ranges from closing opportunity gaps to strengthening staff retention, and he has consulted with school districts around the country on school improvement and family engagement.

Dr. Rivera is a frequent guest speaker and panelist on topics such as equity of access, learning loss during the pandemic, and the important relationship between schools and their communities. He co-authored a report conducted by the Centers for Disease Control and Prevention that studied COVID-19 infections and transmission among elementary educators and students, and based upon Marietta City Schools' approach to the pandemic, he and the district were featured on a "60 Minutes" segment that aired in March 2021. Dr. Rivera serves as a board member of multiple education-focused organizations, and he is actively engaged in raising funds and awareness of pediatric cancer.

David R. Shafer is a successful entrepreneur and business leader anchored primarily in the K-12 market with successes also in the broadcast, entertainment, and banking industries. Mr. Shafer co-founded Frontline Education that today serves over 12,000 school systems. He also was a partner in the company that introduced the Skycam aerial broadcast camera system known throughout the world for covering live sports from above the action. This technology has been recognized with multiple Academy Awards and Emmys.

Mr. Shafer is a passionate advocate for public education serving several terms as an elected School Board Director in Pennsylvania. His community service also includes serving as an Executive Board Member of the Boy Scouts of America (he is an Eagle Scout), several terms on the executive board of the YMCA, and serving on Millersville University of Pennsylvania's Alumni Executive Board. He lives in Royersford, Pennsylvania, with his wife and three children.

Preface

Approaches Running Throughout This Book

School culture, when understood, lays the foundations for creating powerful improvement opportunities through the interactions between school leaders and teachers who now must occupy the shared space and responsibility for culture. This shared space is important because the work and success of schools is directly related to the behaviors, patterns, rituals, and workplace conditions emanating from how people interact with each other. A positive school culture is built through relationships and interactions. Relationships between teachers and students, leaders and teachers, and teachers with their peers influence culture.

In *Leading School Culture through Teacher Voice and Agency*, culture is examined in new ways so that leaders can unpack its influence and the importance of supporting the work of teachers. The book presents a Framework for School Culture that is examined throughout each of the eight chapters. The Framework for School Culture is presented in the image of an iceberg (see Figure 1.1, Chapter 1). This Framework is important as it brings to light that school culture is an untapped resource that can move schools forward only if it is defined and examined through Unifying Elements, acted upon through teacher voice and agency, and jointly connected to build capacity to bring forward collective responsibility.

Objectives of the Book

Our intention for writing *Leading School Culture through Teacher Voice and Agency* was to bring the value of culture to the forefront for teachers and leaders as they navigate the changes needed to improve the achievement for all students. Although schools are steeped in school improvement efforts, the ending results have proven to show nominal outcomes in meeting the goal for all students to succeed. Teachers and leaders across the country want to get it right when students walk through the schoolhouse doors or open a Zoom session. However, after years of high expectations and incredible efforts, schools may be losing ground. Exacerbated by the COVID-19 pandemic and other national crises, schools are seeing more teachers leave the classroom, fewer teachers entering the profession, and school cultures that are growing more toxic by the day. This book posits that culture is the lynchpin in helping schools maintain stability in the midst of internal and external turbulence, change, and during times of innovation.

While school culture has always been important, its value and impact on the work of teachers remains minimized. Its definition continues to be vague and its relationships to school climate blurry. Furthermore, there has been no consistent and driving definition enabling measurement that leads to school and system improvement nor has there been significant and simultaneous efforts to support teachers and leaders as they engage in the work of culture.

The first objective of the book is to bring clarity about school culture by defining and describing culture so leaders can better understand what constitutes a positive culture as illustrated in the Framework for School Culture and the Unifying Elements. Through examining school culture and the unifying elements found within the Framework for School Culture, leaders and teachers can strategically and collectively impact their culture to support their work.

The second objective is to comprehensively articulate how culture can be reshaped through teacher voice and agency to create greater focus on learning for teachers, leaders, and students. The third objective is to explore how culture is impacted by the very ways in which teachers and leaders interact bringing light to workplace conditions, trust, and collaboration. The fourth objective is to underscore the need to create a network of support and the concerted and needed efforts to affirm the work of teachers and the value of being in a community of learners. The fifth objective of the book is to magnify the roles, actions, and responsibilities of teachers and leaders to shape school culture.

The content of the chapters serves to illustrate how school culture is ever changing due to the relational dynamics between leaders and teachers and the importance of culture related to teacher induction, growth, and retention. A positive school culture cannot be mandated through legislation because it evolves from the interactions and the experiences of teachers who want to be empowered to do their very best work.

Book Features

There are several hands-on features in *Leading School Culture through Teacher Voice and Agency* to support the application of the concepts presented across the chapters. In the first chapter, the Framework for School Culture and the Unifying Elements are presented. This framework and the unifying elements are unpacked across the chapters.

Each chapter starts with an opening scenario, *Examining School Culture*. This scenario situates the content of the chapter as a dilemma of practice that the reader can track while reading. Like a smart word problem in math, sufficiently identified concepts that are amplified in the chapter are embedded.

At the end of each chapter section, a recap of major take-aways from that section, *Leading Culture*, focuses the reader on applying principles of culture to the dilemma of practice presented in the chapter lead off, *Examining School Culture*.

Each chapter culminates with a section entitled, *Leading Practices*, to engage the reader to pull out strategies that can be adapted to the context in which the reader leads. These strategies pull from the major content of the book and build deeper levels of understanding (knowing) of the chapter content to activities that would broadly engage the reader in planning, implementing, and/or assessing key areas aspects related to school culture.

Suggested readings are offered to support learning more about specific areas of school culture.

What's Inside the Chapters

The content of *Leading School Culture through Teacher Voice and Agency* spans eight chapters. The chapter annotations serve to acquaint the reader with the contents of each.

Chapter 1: Teacher Voice and Agency

Leveraging the power of school culture requires educators in schools to be engaged. Their roles, responsibilities, and abilities jointly need to move to collective responsibility that is foundational to building a healthy and stable culture. The Framework for School Culture and the Unifying Elements are presented in the form of an iceberg that serves to anchor teacher voice and agency as the foundation needed to build collective responsibility within the school.

- Framework for School Culture
- Clarity about Teacher Voice and Agency
  - Teacher Voice Defined
  - Teacher Agency Defined
- Teachers as Culture Leaders
  - Making the Connections to Support Teachers
  - Empowerment Then
  - Empowerment Now
  - Autonomy
  - Self-Efficacy
  - Collective Efficacy

Chapter 2: Understanding and Framing School Culture

School culture, often used interchangeably with school climate, continues to be a point of conversation in schools; yet, its definitions and components remain vague. The power of a healthy and vibrant organizational and school culture does not just "happen."

- Culture and Climate Differ
  - Culture Defined
  - Climate Defined
- Internal Factors that Influence School Culture
  - Teachers
  - Workplace Conditions

- Teacher Morale
- Levels of Engagement
- Teacher Retention and Attrition
- Leader Mobility
- External Factors that Influence School Culture
  - Poverty
  - Shifting Demographics
  - Student Mobility and Attrition
  - Divisive Political Environments

Chapter 3: Understanding Functional and Dysfunctional Cultures

Understanding the dynamics and levels of functionality of culture remains essential as schools rely on its power to improve the work of teachers and leaders. Important for leaders is understanding their role in leading culture and the characteristics of functional and dysfunctional school cultures.

- Leading with a Culture Vision
  - Understanding the Culture
  - Culture Leaders
  - Leading with a Culture Lens
- Functional Culture and Climate
  - Positive Culture and Climate
  - Positive Culture and Climate Intersect
  - Key Norms Support Positive School Culture and Climate
- Dysfunctional Culture and Climate
  - Dynamics
  - Collegiality and Collaboration
- Changing the Culture Vision
  - Reculturing
  - Leading "Good" Disturbance
  - Stabilizing School Culture

Chapter 4: Transforming School Culture Is a Human Endeavor

Focusing on developing school culture requires leaders and teachers to have clarity in its definition as well as an understanding of its presence within the school. While school culture is often described in various ways across schools, there are conditions that must serve to support the working relationships between teachers and leaders.

- Relationships Matter
  - Care and Support
  - Normative Behaviors Send Explicit Messages
  - The Lonely Road of Isolation
  - Affiliation and Sense of Belonging
- Collaborative Structures
  - Making Practice Public
  - Teacher Leadership
  - Professional Learning Communities
  - Online Learning Communities
  - Collaborative Planning
  - Mentoring and Induction

Chapter 5: Professional Learning Cultures Grow People and Systems

While effective professional learning has been central to improving teacher and leader effectiveness, its importance, as well as delivery, has not always impacted practices. Creating a culture of professional engagement requires new mindsets in professional delivery, support of new practices, and an understanding of its impact on the system.

- Collaboration
  - Bringing Clarity to Collaboration
  - Leading a Collaborative Learning Culture
  - Creating a Collaborative Learning Culture

- Professional Learning
  - Unpacking Professional Learning
  - Focusing on Professional Job-embedded Learning
  - Promoting Supportive Collaborative Practices

Chapter 6: The Social Dynamics That Build School Culture

With the increased intensity of school disruptions and its impact on teachers, leaders must pivot their focus to the human capital within the system and the culture in which they work. Creating processes to build a culture on the foundations of teacher ownership and collective responsibility will be critical for leaders moving forward to support them and build the capacity to improve schools.

- School Capacity
  - Collective Ownership
  - Collective Responsibility
  - Coherence
- Human Capital
  - Induction
  - Mentoring
  - Teacher Leadership
- Social Capital
  - Relationship to Human Capital
  - Social Networks

Chapter 7: Leveraging Culture to Stabilize the School House

School leaders and teachers will need to navigate a changing school culture in readying for the ongoing turbulence and disruptions from outside and within the system. The new normal for school culture will evolve by acknowledging change processes and ensuring levels of resiliency—both central as education is reshaped.

- Culture, Turbulence, and Disruption
  - Turbulence
  - External Turbulence
  - Internal Turbulence
  - Personal and Professional Turbulence
- Readying for Tomorrow Through Culture
  - Leading Through Cultural Turbulence
  - Stabilizing Through Unifying Elements
  - Impact of Subcultures
- Culture in the New School House
  - School Culture Expanded
  - Culture Tensions
  - New Focus

Chapter 8: It's All About Culture

This chapter highlights the major take-aways from the first seven chapters and offers final perspectives about school personnel to work continuously at building a culture that embraces learning for all.

- Revisiting the Framework for School Culture
- Unifying Elements of School Culture
  - Empowerment
  - Autonomy
  - Collaboration
  - Support, Care, and Safety
  - Sense of Belonging
  - Self and Collective Efficacy
  - Professional Engagement
- Asking, Why Culture Now

- Culture Supports Teachers
  - Teacher Effectiveness
  - Teacher Retention
  - Professional Learning
  - Work-place Conditions
  - Collective Responsibility and Ownership
  - Human and Social Capital
- Key Takeaways About School Culture

Acknowledgements

As a team, we are thankful for the good will of many who contributed behind the scenes to this effort. There are two individuals whose dedication and work ethic helped to keep this project on schedule—Dr. Sevda Yildirim and Dr. Salih Cevik—both who earned their Ph.D.'s in Educational Administration and Policy at the University of Georgia in 2022 and who now are policy analysts back in their home country, Turkey. Sevda and Salih worked tirelessly. We are indebted to these scholars and their concerted efforts as they completed their doctoral studies at the University of Georgia.

We are appreciative of Mr. Dan Roth, Owner and Art Director of Athens Creative Design, LLC. Dan brought to life Figure 1.1 that represents the Framework for School Culture and its Unifying Elements. This figure serves to anchor our examination of school culture and the primacy of teacher voice and agency as its foundation. Dan, your artistic and trained eye for detail and perfection supported our efforts to get the words right.

Without saying, we are humbled by the good will of Heather Jarrow, Senior Editor with the Routledge/Taylor and Francis Group. Heather's keen intellect helped us bring clarity to purpose through her feedback on the original book proposal. We are appreciative of your quick response—even during a pandemic. Also, a special thank you to Rebecca Collazo, Editorial Assistant, Education, who helped in so many ways through her organization and eye to detail.

Thank you,

Sally J. Zepeda, Ph.D.
Philip D. Lanoue, Ph.D.
Grant M. Rivera, Ed.D.
David R. Shafer

Teacher Voice and Agency

In This Chapter . . .

 ## Examining School Culture

A new superintendent was hired in a district of 50,000 students knowing that one of the significant concerns expressed throughout the interview process and reflected from numerous documents was the lack of teacher

DOI: 10.4324/9781003222651-1

engagement in school improvement efforts. A major take-away was there existed a "bunker mentality" culture where teachers work in isolation.

To better understand the needs of schools and needed improvements, the superintendent established a teacher advisory council with members representing every school in the district. The Council was to meet quarterly with members of the central office cabinet to discuss concerns and opportunities for improvements. The agenda for each meeting was developed through teacher and cabinet input.

The teacher's interests for the first meeting were mostly focused on moving out of isolation and having a louder voice in the decision-making processes and greater latitude in decision making at the school and classroom levels. Teachers in every school indicated that they did not want a "script" on how to teach or for making decisions in their schools.

The superintendent embraced the concept of building a district culture of empowerment through teacher voice and agency, and she believed this was the foundation for the ownership needed to move the system forward with changes in policies and practices. After the first Council meeting, the superintendent decided to create a working committee comprised of teachers and school and district leaders to develop a framework for schools to create

1. A definition of teacher voice and teacher agency.
2. New constructs to support teacher empowerment, autonomy, and self-efficacy.
3. A process and timeline to review existing procedures and to develop new ones. procedures and policies to ensure alignment.

Introduction

In a time where unparalleled change is upon the entire educational system, school improvement efforts, both locally and nationally, have painfully delivered relatively flat results. The impact of school culture continues to be a relatively elusive element in improving schools across the country. While school improvement efforts nationally and locally have garnered a much-needed focus on connecting effective instructional practices to student achievement, immense challenges continue to exist. The unique and untapped power of a school's culture remains disconnected from assisting school improvement efforts. Although school culture is examined fully in Chapter 2, it is characterized as the personality of the school built on the beliefs and values embedded in a "strong supportive environment, [where] the level of autonomy is high, and sharing and collaboration are its basis" (Cansoy & Parlar, 2017, p. 312).

Leveraging the power of school culture requires educators in schools to be engaged and working together collectively. There are many moving parts associated with a school's culture. To capture these moving parts, this book lays the foundation for creating school cultures through the interactions between school leaders and teachers who occupy shared spaces. This chapter presents the Framework for School Culture and focuses primarily on two foundational aspects of school culture, teacher voice and agency and the interplay between them and other unifying elements embedded in the Framework.

Framework for School Culture

A Framework for School Culture in Figure 1.1 is presented in the form of an iceberg that serves to anchor teacher voice and agency as the foundation needed to build collective responsibility within the school. School climate is at the tip, its most visible point. Below school climate is the space where school culture resides. Next is the waterline. Looking below the waterline and spiraling upward are a series of unifying elements: sense of belonging; support, care, and safety; autonomy; self-efficacy; collective efficacy; empowerment; and professional engagement. These unifying elements are what, for the most part, make a school culture what it is and leads teachers and leaders to collective responsibility and action.

This Framework for School Culture is an important one that will be referenced throughout the chapters. Figure 1.1 illustrates:

- the position of teacher voice and agency is *the* foundation of school culture. Teacher voice and agency not only serve as cultural anchors, but they also create the synergy for the movement within the unifying elements;
- the unifying elements are embedded in a culture;
- the dynamic nature of the unifying elements impact school culture—positive or negative;
- the unifying elements are not hierarchical or linear in that their ordering occurs above, below, and/or at the same level with each other; and,
- the unifying elements do not exist in a "black box" in that they interact and influence each one in very unpredictable ways that are embedded and specific to the context of the school.

Framework for School Culture

Figure 1.1 Framework for School Culture

School culture much like a majority of an iceberg is *below* the surface whereas climate emanates outwardly, as in the "tip of an iceberg."

Key to the analogy of Figure 1.1 is that unless you are *intentionally looking below the surface*, you won't see what or how all of these incredibly critical unifying elements can be pulled together to improve a school's culture. To point, climate surfaces as the most outwardly visible factors—behaviors, patterns, rituals, workplace conditions—that emanate from within the culture, based in part, on how people interact with one another.

There is great interplay between the unifying elements found within most school cultures. This interplay is dynamic, constantly ebbing and flowing. This ebb and flow follow changes for a variety of reasons including school personnel (hiring new teachers to replace retiring ones), demographic shifts (students and community), and new site and system leadership.

The dynamics between the unifying elements influence one another and can create tensions. For example, collaboration is a unifying element that impacts culture. Consider the dynamic between promoting autonomy and collaboration where leaders want teachers to work in teams, but they also want teachers to be independent, to make judgments, and to enact improvements based on the needs of students in their *own* classrooms. If a culture is strong and positive, it can thrive through the endless possibilities that these tensions create. In fact, lurking within these tensions are where solutions emerge and where the convergence of multiple perspectives evolve.

The foundation of a powerfully strong and active school culture that fully supports all is created systemically through teacher voice and agency. Therefore, clarity is needed to understand the importance and role of teacher voice and agency in improving school culture.

Clarity About Teacher Voice and Agency

Teaching, learning, and leading are highly complex, and the work of leading schools can no longer be solely vested in the principal. Voice and agency help to build strong cultures where teachers are engaged in the work of learning and growing both in classrooms and among their peers. As the most valuable resources in a school, teachers have expertise that can serve as an asset. It is one thing to have expertise, but it's what happens as a result of this expertise that counts, more, in building and sustaining a culture where teachers feel that they belong, that they make a difference, and that what they say and think are valued.

Strong school leadership has always remained incredibly important for highly functioning and continuously improving schools. While school culture is indeed shared by teachers and leaders, the role of the leader to support and foster a continuous process of improvement remains critical. As a school leader, it is hardly possible to support a positive school culture if teacher voice and agency are not exerted. Leveraging the power of teacher voice and agency opens up opportunities for improving schools differently from past practices predicated on top-down leadership approaches. Through teacher voice and agency, systems can develop the culture required for systemic and sustained change that fuels school improvement.

Teacher voice and agency are interrelated concepts that teachers experience, develop, and enact within the very specific contexts of schools. Teacher voice and agency do not stand alone. Referring back to Figure 1.1, there are numerous unifying elements such as a sense of belonging, autonomy, and others. These unifying elements interact and influence one another. The safe but monolithic approach is to try to put these unifying elements in a black box, so they are self-contained. These unifying elements are messy and recursive, and they depend on many workplace conditions, patterns of interaction, and the beliefs and attitudes of teachers and leaders.

One would think that teacher voice and agency as a precursor to the development of culture rests on a slippery slope. Slow down. There are basic premises about teacher voice and agency that lay the foundation for the work that school leaders and teachers need to engage in to continuously build up their school's culture. Voice is the gateway to teacher agency, autonomy, and empowerment.

Teacher Voice Defined

Throughout eras of accountability, teachers were positioned at "the endpoint of educational reform; the last to hear, the last to know, the last to speak. They are mainly the objects of reform, not its participants" (Hargreaves & Shirley, 2011, p. 1). Teacher voice is often thought to be silenced, even neglected both in literature and in policy-making (Gozali et al., 2017). The meaning of teacher voice is important to understand given its relevant importance to school culture.

Teacher voice has been examined extensively in the literature with very nuanced definitions that have changed over time. In practice, however, the conditions in which teacher voice and agency unfold are identified. The Quaglia Institute (2020) offers an applied definition:

> **Voice** is sharing thoughts and ideas in an environment underpinned by trust and respect, offering realistic suggestions for the good of the whole, and accepting responsibility for not only what is said but also what needs to be done.
>
> (p. 1, emphasis in the original)

This definition includes such words as "trust" and "respect" pointing to the ways in which teachers and leaders treat one another. There are phrases that describe certain actions such as "accepting responsibility" that lead from individual to a collective "good of the whole."

Through teacher engagement, schools are able to harness the knowledge and experience from its teacher base in ways to improve (Coutts, 2018). Moreover, "as teachers discover the power of their own voices, they are able to re-envision their roles as critical educators who empower their own students" (View & DeMulder, 2009, p. 35). Further, when teachers experience improvements developed through their voice it perpetuates continuous improvement.

Leaders are now realizing that teachers who exert their voices work in very purposeful ways to leverage individual and collective efforts to improve their classroom practices and to collaboratively work with other teachers. Leaders support teachers in developing their voices when they create opportunities to lead curricular, instructional, and professional development efforts, and to collaborate on the formulation of school policy and procedures.

Voice is important for other reasons. In their Voice Framework, the Quaglia Institute (2020) asserts that the guiding principle of self-worth is achieved, in part, when teachers and leaders promote belonging in an environment where teachers derive a sense of accomplishment from their work (see also Figure 1.1). Without this sense of accomplishment, teachers are more often poised to leave the profession, adding to the deleterious impact of attrition of up to 50% of any entering cohort by the fifth year. Schools will be more successful when leaders recognize not only the value of voice, but also are able to connect voice with teacher agency—the actions stemming from voice.

Teacher Agency Defined

Teacher agency creates the context to move from voice to the ability to *act*. Teacher agency has been conceived in a variety of ways in the literature from both individual and collective lenses in which teachers engage through their actions, reflections, and relationships. Biesta et al. (2017) viewed agency as teachers "exerting control over and giving direction to their everyday practices, bearing in mind that such practices are not just the outcome of teachers' judgements and actions, but are also shaped by the structured cultures within which teachers work" (p. 39). Hökkä et al. (2017) asserts that collective agency occurs when "*professional communities exert influence, make choices, and take stances in ways that affect their work and their professional identities*" (p. 38, emphasis in the original).

As an iterative process, agency evolves over time and is shaped by beliefs and values (Emirbayer & Mische, 1998). To exercise agency, teachers must

- possess a sense of purpose and the belief that they can exert influence about this purpose (King & Nomikou, 2018; Pantic, 2017);
- gather resources, take action, and engage in risk taking, supported through relationships (Hökkä et al., 2017; Pantic, 2017);
- continue to reflect about actions, choices, and beliefs (Bandura, 2006; Biesta et al., 2017; Tao & Gao, 2017); and,
- feel autonomous and empowered to be able to act with confidence (Molla & Nolan, 2020; Pantic, 2017).

Agency "is about the relations between actors and the environments in and through which they act" (Biesta et al., 2017, p. 40)—all embedded in a school's culture. Agency occurs when teachers can "(a) make autonomous decisions, (b) base the decisions on deliberation about purpose and value,

(c) act in light of their decisions, and (d) bring about changes in their practice" (Molla & Nolan, 2020, p. 72).

These ideas about agency are congruent with what we know about the adult learner and parallel the theories supporting job-embedded professional learning (Zepeda, 2019). Teacher agency in the field of professional learning has steadily and consistently evolved as teachers seek to improve their instructional expertise (Calvert, 2016; Molla & Nolan, 2020; Philpott & Oates, 2017; Zepeda, 2015, 2019). From this lens, teacher agency is *"the capacity of teachers to act purposefully and constructively to direct their professional growth and contribute to the growth of their colleagues"* (Calvert, 2016, p. 4, emphasis in the original).

In a learning culture, teachers are engaged in collaborative efforts, and are committed to acting on 1) their beliefs, 2) their experiences, and 3) the knowledge that is co-constructed with others (see Chapter 5). Individual and collective agency can only flourish in a culture that supports teacher decision-making and their efforts for improving their practices (Zepeda, 2018). At the forefront of such a culture is a foundation of trust. Teachers need and want to be "trusted to take risks" (Hauserman & Stick, 2013, p. 196). According to Tschannen-Moran (2014),

> principals and teachers who trust each other can better work together in the service of solving the challenging problems of schooling. These leaders create a bond that helps to inspire teachers to move to a higher level of effort and achievement.
>
> (p. 13)

Leading Culture

Creating Teacher Voice and Teacher Agency

- School culture is built on leveraging the power of teacher voice and agency.
- Voice occurs when teachers share thoughts and ideas in an environment of mutual trust and respect.
- Agency is the transition from voice to action whereby teachers are empowered to act purposely and constructively.

Supporting Teacher Voice and Agency

- Identify and describe how teachers are given voice in your school.
- How does teacher voice lead to creating change?
- What processes exist or are needed in your school to leverage teacher agency?

To leverage teachers' voice and agency, leaders must also examine school culture and the underlying, overlapping, and overall principles about empowerment, autonomy, self-efficacy, and collective efficacy. This work is centered on developing teachers as leaders of culture.

Teachers as Culture Leaders

To build culture, leaders must be in a position to create the right workplace conditions with a focus on the aspects that either act as barriers or provide the support for teachers as they grow as professionals. Teachers are best positioned to be culture leaders when they are

- empowered;
- able to act on their own critical judgements about their work (autonomy);
- involved in shaping school policy and procedures;
- engaged in decision making;
- encouraged to collaborate with others in shared spaces; and,
- holding the belief that they can be successful (self-efficacy), and that school improvement stems from believing that collective voices and actions lead to success (collective efficacy).

Teachers are the real culture leaders in their schools. Think about the visibility that teachers have. They are at the front-line holding responsibility for the students entrusted to their care. They carry forward the mission of the school, and they communicate broadly in the communities in which they work. Teachers are the torch-bearers for the work of educating students and advocating for resources to do so.

Teachers can influence a culture both inside and outside of their classrooms through their interactions with students, colleagues, school leaders, and members of the community. School leaders who embrace teacher voice are able to promote agency required in building culture leaders who are responsive to the ever-changing needs of the school and its communities.

To be strategic, school leaders need to understand and expand teachers' influence on the impact of school culture. The first step is recognizing the connections between empowerment, autonomy, self-efficacy, and collective efficacy to realize "the collective influence of teachers who function as empowered professionals" (Marks & Louis, 1999, p. 708). Furthermore, Killion et al. (2016) asserts the importance for leaders to understand the elements of a healthy school culture—relational trust, collective responsibility, commitment to continuous development, recognition, and autonomy.

Making the Connections to Support Teachers

Revisiting Figure 1.1 and a review of the literature illustrate the connections between *empowerment, autonomy, self-efficacy*, and *collective efficacy* as they relate to teacher voice, agency, and school culture. There is considerable overlap between these constructs as illustrated in Figure 1.2.

To understand the ways that these constructs overlap, each will be examined offering definitions and making the connections to culture and practice. These constructs are messy, recursive, and illustrate that school culture must be contextualized considering such variables as the characteristics of teachers and their relative experience levels; past history of leadership approaches; and the existing culture at the school site.

Empowerment Then

Teacher empowerment in schools has evolved from earlier years where the focus was part of movements such as reforming and restructuring schools (Lieberman & Miller, 1990; Sarason, 1992), a means to enact transformative

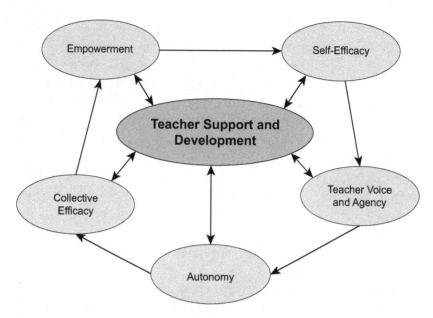

Figure 1.2 Overlapping Constructs Needed to Support Teacher Development

leadership to improve schools (Duke, 1987), and ways to promote teacher leadership (Boles & Troen, 1992; Owens, 2004). These efforts led to casting new roles for teachers to be decision makers on policies and practices (Marks & Louis, 1997; Short & Rinehart, 1992; Wasley, 1991), to gain and develop competence (Short, 1994), and to enact the working conditions that foster collegiality and teamwork nestled in safe spaces for teachers to collaborate (Rosenholtz, 1991).

Empowerment, for the most part, was bypassed most notably during the No Child Left Behind (NCLB, 2002) era marked by accountability through standardized tests, national benchmarks, and more scripted curriculum, pacing guides, and routinization of instruction to deliver it (Pinar, 2012). Empowerment was replaced by teacher evaluation systems predicated on value-added measures that kept administrators and teachers fixated on linking individual student outcomes. Essentially, a large portion of a teacher's effectiveness hinged on how well their students performed based on predetermined measures of teacher effectiveness that varied by state, often with limited ability to make classroom and school wide decisions.

Empowerment Now

With the movement toward more decentralization from the federal government and the reauthorization of the Elementary and Secondary Education Act (e.g., Every Student Succeeds Act of, 2015) on such matters as teacher evaluation and professional development, some of the metrics used to measure teachers have lessened, giving them and leaders the space to engage in conversations about teaching and learning. Professional learning communities and the emergence of teacher leaders who fulfill key roles as instructional coaches have served as vehicles to engage and to empower teachers to lead conversations and to make decisions that support student learning.

The COVID-19 global pandemic changed the face of school and its rituals, giving way to new technologies with teachers pivoting the ways they teach, interact with colleagues, and make decisions about the curriculum and its instructional delivery (Zepeda & Lanoue, 2021). Teachers carried the day as did school leaders as critical decisions were often made in a matter of hours. School cultures and workplace conditions changed with no forewarning. Constant pivots with learning options had teachers planning around the clock often in isolations while balancing their work and home-life as best as possible. The core principles of school culture were challenged with much turbulence as the conditions needed for safety continuously impacted educational decisions along the way. Today, empowerment is being reshaped and defined.

Empowerment Defined

Promoting empowerment is an investment in building capacity because "Empowered individuals believe they have the skills and knowledge to act on a situation and improve it" (Short, 1994, p. 488). The base of empowerment "refers to the opportunities a person has for autonomy, responsibility, choice, and authority" (Lightfoot, 1986, p. 9). As Figure 1.2 illustrates, empowerment overlaps with many of the unifying elements of a school culture as depicted in Figure 1.1.

Empowerment is not linear but rather it is a multi-dimensional process as envisioned by Short (1994) whose corpus of work identifies six dimensions of empowerment as illustrated in Table 1.1.

Table 1.1 Dimensions of Empowerment

Dimensions of Empowerment	Description
Decision making	Teachers have the authority to make decisions about issues that affect their work, and they have the agency to enact changes associated with them.
Teacher impact	Teachers believe their work will impact students and the school.
Teacher status	Teachers feel respected for their professional expertise by their colleagues and school leaders.
Autonomy in the job	Teachers have the sense that they have freedom to make decisions and to enact change
Opportunities for professional growth	Professional growth is highly personalized. Teachers have a choice and believe their school offers opportunities to continue learning.
Teacher self-efficacy	Teachers believe they can be successful in their work because they have the knowledge and skills to help students learn.

Source: Adapted from Short (1994); Short and Rinehart (1992)

Empowerment is important for school improvement because "teachers who perceive a greater sense of empowerment believe that they can impact the work of the organization and recognize that they have the power to identify problems, institute change efforts, and ultimately, be responsible for organizational outcomes" (Short & Rinehart, 1992, p. 13). Empowered teachers "have a broader *voice* in educational affairs" that lead to effective school improvement decisions (Harpell & Andrews, 2010, p. 191, emphasis added).

Across the literature, the benefits of empowering teachers have been consistent. Empowerment can

- support organizational and professional commitment and citizenship behaviors in schools (Bolger & Somech, 2004);
- lead to higher levels of job-satisfaction (Bolger & Nir, 2012);
- promote risk-taking (Trust, 2017);

- foster collaboration (Balyer et al., 2017); and
- promote teacher leadership (Avidov-Ungar & Arviv-Elyashiv, 2018).

Leaders go a long way to support empowerment by sharing authority over decisions at the classroom level and promoting teacher input in larger issues such as policy and procedure formulation. Throughout this discussion, there have been overlapping concepts identified, including autonomy, self-efficacy, and collective efficacy.

Autonomy

Autonomy is a dimension of empowerment that signals that teachers have influence and control over their work, including, for example, making decisions about their schedules, textbooks, and the curriculum. Teachers who are autonomous have a high degree of control over issues that are connected to their daily work. Autonomy is the cornerstone for teachers to have the discretion to "change things up" to meet the needs of their students and to better control for outcomes. Teachers who have autonomy pursue opportunities that enable them to learn, to grow as professionals, and to exercise agency.

Autonomy signals independence, responsibility, and the discretion to make decisions (Honig & Rainey, 2012; Strong & Yoshida, 2014). Furthermore, Ingersoll and May (2011) found that an increased sense of autonomy leads to lower teacher attrition rates, and decreased levels of autonomy leads to lower job satisfaction (Torres, 2014).

System policies, union agreements, and other structures can often limit the level of autonomy teachers can enact. Balyer et al. (2017) addressed empowerment through the lens of autonomy and self-efficacy. When granted autonomy, teachers are more likely to take risks and to develop their skills because they display self-efficacy—the beliefs that they can be successful.

Teachers develop autonomy as they move through their careers; therefore, it is essential for leaders to know their teachers and their professional growth needs. Sehrawat (2014) further details that teacher autonomy is driven by a need for personal and professional improvement. To promote teacher autonomy, leaders and teachers need to embrace and understand that:

- Teacher autonomy is essential for ensuring a learning environment that addresses children's diverse needs.

- Teacher autonomy is driven by a need for personal and professional improvement, so that an autonomous teacher may seek out opportunities over the course of his/her career to develop further.

- An autonomous teacher feels personal responsibilities, attends workshops, and comes up with new classroom ideas.

- Teacher autonomy refers to the ability to develop appropriate skills, knowledge, and attitude for oneself as a teacher, in cooperation with others.

- The teacher should have the freedom to innovate, to devise appropriate methods of communication, and activities relevant to the needs and capabilities of the concerns of the community.

- Autonomous teachers feel more confident with a virtual learning environment.

- Teacher autonomy is necessary in order to be able to respond to student needs, interests and motivation and to individualize approaches.

(p. 8)

A belief in oneself, known as self-efficacy, shapes autonomy and gives the voice needed to generate the momentum for teacher agency.

Self-Efficacy

Bandura's (1997) work positions self-efficacy as the "beliefs in one's capabilities to organize and execute the courses of action required to produce given attainments" (p. 3). In the context of education, Tschannen-Moran et al. (1998) defined teacher efficacy as "the teacher's belief in his or her capability to organize and execute courses of action required to successfully accomplish a specific teaching task in a particular context" (p. 233).

For school leaders working with teachers, the following are important considerations:

- Self-efficacy for educators is not a fixed concept (Yoo, 2016) in that it changes over time. One factor that can have a positive effect on self-efficacy is professional development.

- Culture impacts self-efficacy. When leaders create a supportive culture, teachers' self-efficacy improves, as does overall job satisfaction (Aldridge & Fraser, 2016; Hallinger et al., 2018).

Collective Efficacy

Collective efficacy is defined as the sense that teachers as a group believe they can accomplish given tasks together. Goddard and Goddard (2001) assert that "where teachers tend to think highly of the collective capability of the faculty, they may sense an expectation for successful teaching and hence work to be successful themselves" (pp. 815–816). Moreover, teacher collective efficacy is essential to building a culture where all students can succeed regardless of factors "over and above the educational impact of their homes and communities" (Tschannen-Moran & Barr, 2004, p. 190).

Leading Culture

Creating Teacher Empowerment, Autonomy, Self-efficacy, and Collective Efficacy

- Teachers who are empowered can impact school culture by identifying problems and instituting positive change.
- Autonomy allows teachers to have a high degree of freedom in making decisions connected to their daily work.
- Efficacy is developed when individual teachers and the larger collective of teachers believe they have the ability to create meaningful change.

Supporting Teacher Empowerment, Autonomy, Self-efficacy, and Collective Efficacy

- Explain how empowerment is defined, enacted, and embraced in your school.
- What processes are in place to support teachers and collective autonomy?
- In what ways have teacher empowerment and autonomy contributed to building self and collective-efficacy?

Chapter Summary

The success of any school with rise and fall on school culture and climate. Like an iceberg, school culture lives below the surface; school climate emanates outwardly as the "tip of the iceberg." School culture is developed through intentional, strategic, and consistent actions and decisions by school leaders, the most important of which are teacher voice and agency.

Teacher voice and agency encompass elements of empowerment, autonomy, and self- and collective-efficacy. Each school leader must do their own reflective "gut check" on their understanding of teacher voice and agency. The elements of teacher voice and agency must be consistently defined, prioritized, and measured. School leaders can't lead this work if they don't understand it and, truth be told, there is little margin for error or experimentation.

Leading Practices

1. *Analyzing* teacher voice and agency in your school
    a. In a process involving all faculty, create a definition of voice and agency for your school.
2. *Developing Processes* around teacher voice and agency
    a. With your faculty, identify processes that either support or hinder these definitions.
3. *Implementing Strategies* to leverage teacher voice and agency
    a. How would you create opportunities for teachers to be engaged based on their interests, areas of expertise, and the needs of the school?

Suggested Readings

Durrant, J. (2020). *Teacher agency, professional development and school improvement*. Routledge.

Good, A. G. (2018). *Teachers at the table: Voice, agency, and advocacy in educational policymaking*. Rowman & Littlefield.

Quaglia, R. J., & Lande, L. L. (2016). *Teacher voice: Amplifying success*. Corwin Press.

References

Aldridge, J. M., & Fraser, B. J. (2016). Teachers' views of their school climate and its relationship with teacher self-efficacy and job satisfaction. *Learning Environments Research, 19*(2), 291–307. https://doi.org/10.1007/s10984-015-9198-x

Avidov-Ungar, A., & Arviv-Elyashiv, R. (2018). Teacher perceptions of empowerment and promotion during reforms. *International Journal of Educational Management, 32*(1), 155–170. https://doi.org/10.1108/IJEM-01-2017-0002

Balyer, A., Özcan, K., & Yildiz, A. (2017). Teacher empowerment: School administrator roles. *Eurasian Journal of Educational Research, 70*(1), 1–18. http://ejer.com.tr

Bandura, A. (1997). *Self-efficacy: The exercise of control.* W.H. Freeman and Company.

Bandura, A. (2006). Toward a psychology of human agency: Perspectives on psychological science. *Association for Psychological Science, 1*(2), 164–180. https://doi.org/10.1111/j.1745-6916.2006.00011.x

Biesta, G., Priestley, M., & Robinson, S. (2017). Talking about education: Exploring the significance of teachers' talk for teacher agency. *Journal of Curriculum Studies, 49*(1), 38–54. https://doi.org/10.1080/00220272.2016.1205143

Boles, K., & Troen, V. (1992). How teachers make restructuring happen. *Educational Leadership, 49*(5), 53–56. www.ascd.org/publications/educational-leadership.aspx

Bolger, R., & Nir, A. E. (2012). The importance of teachers' perceived organizational support to job satisfaction: What's empowerment got to do with it? *Journal of Educational Administration, 50*(3), 287–206. https://doi.org/10.1108/09578231211223310

Bolger, R., & Somech, A. (2004). Influence of teacher empowerment on teachers' organizational commitment, professional commitment and organizational citizenship behavior in schools. *Teaching and Teacher Education, 20*(2004), 277–289. https://doi.org/10.1016/j.tate.2004.02.003

Calvert, L. (2016). Moving from compliance to agency: What teachers need to make professional learning work. *Learning Forward.* https://learningforward.org/publications/teacher-agency

Cansoy, R., & Parlar, H. (2017). Examining the relationship between school culture and teacher leadership. *International Online Journal of Educational Sciences, 9*(2), 310–322. https://iojes.net

Coutts, N. (2018, April). Teacher agency vs the collective voice. *The Learners Way*. https://thelearnersway.net/ideas/2018/4/22/teacher-agency-vs-the-collective-voice

Duke, D. L. (1987). *School leadership and instructional improvement*. Random House Inc.

Emirbayer, M., & Mische, A. (1998). What is agency? *American Journal of Sociology, 103*(4), 962–1023. https://doi.org/10.1086/231294

ESSA. (2015). Every Student Succeeds Act of 2015, Pub. L. No. 114–95 § 114 Stat. 1177 (2015–2016). www.ed.gov/essa

Goddard, R. D., & Goddard, Y. L. (2001). A multilevel analysis of the relationship between teacher and collective efficacy in urban schools. *Teaching and Teacher Education, 17*(7), 807–818. https://doi.org/10.1016/S0742-051X(01)00032-4

Gozali, C., Thrush, E. C., Soto-Peña, Whang, C., & Luschei, T. F. (2017). Teacher voice in global conversations around educational access, equity, and quality. *FIRE: Forum for International Research in Education, 4*(1), 32–51.

Hallinger, P., Hosseingholizadeh, R., Hashemi, N., & Kouhsari, M. (2018). Do beliefs make a difference? Exploring how principal self-efficacy and instructional leadership impact teacher efficacy and commitment in Iran. *Educational Management Administration & Leadership, 46*(5), 800–819. https://doi.org/10.1177/1741143217700283

Hargreaves, A., & Shirley, D. (2011). The far side of educational reform. *Canadian Teachers' Federation*. www.ctf-fce.ca

Harpell, J. V., & Andrews, J. J. (2010). Administrative leadership in the age of inclusion: Promoting best practices and teacher empowerment. *The Journal of Educational Thought (JET)/Revue De La Pensée Éducative, 44*(2), 189–210. www.jstor.org/stable/23767214

Hauserman, C. P., & Stick, S. L. (2013). The leadership teachers want from principals: Transformational. *Canadian Journal of Education, 36*(3), 184–203. https://cje-rce.ca/

Hökkä, P., Vähäsantanen, K., & Mahlakaarto, S. (2017). Teacher educators' collective professional agency and identity—transforming marginality to strength. *Teaching and Teacher Education*, *63*(2017), 36–46. https://doi.org/10.1016/j.tate.2016.12.001

Honig, M. I., & Rainey, L. R. (2012). Autonomy and school improvement: What do we know and where do we go from here? *Educational Policy*, *26*(3), 465–495. https://doi.org/10.1177/0895904811417590

Ingersoll, R. M., & May, H. (2011). The minority teacher shortage: Fact or fable? *The Phi Delta Kappan*, *93*(1), 62–65. https://kappanonline.org

Killion, J., Harrison, C., Colton, A., Bryan, C., Delehant, A., & Cooke, D. (2016). *A systemic approach to elevating teacher leadership*. Leaning Forward.

King, H., & Nomikou, E. (2018). Fostering critical teacher agency: The impact of a science capital pedagogical approach. *Pedagogy, Culture & Society*, *26*(1), 87–103. https://doi.org/10.1080/14681366.2017.1353539

Lieberman, A., & Miller, L. (1990). Restructuring schools: What matters and what works. *Phi Delta Kappan*, *71*, 750–764. https://kappanonline.org

Lightfoot, S. L. (1986). On goodness of schools: Themes of empowerment. *Peabody Journal of Education*, *63*(3), 9–28. https://doi.org/10.1080/01619568609538522

Marks, H. M., & Louis, K. S. (1997). Does teacher empowerment affect the classroom? The implications of teacher empowerment for instruction practice and student academic performance. *Educational Evaluation and Policy Analysis*, *9*(3), 245–275. https://doi.org/10.3102/01623737019003245

Marks, H. M., & Louis, K. S. (1999). Teacher empowerment and the capacity for organizational learning. *Educational Administration Quarterly*, *35*(5), 707–750. https://doi.org/10.1177/0013161X99355003

Molla, T., & Nolan, A. (2020). Teacher agency and professional practice. *Teachers and Teaching*, *26*(1), 67–87. https://doi.org/10.1080/13540602.2020.1740196

No Child Left Behind Act of 2002, Public Law PL 107–110. (2002). www2.ed.gov/policy/elsec/leg/esea02/107-110.pdf

Owens, R. (2004). *Organization behavior in education: Adaptive leadership and school reform* (8th ed.). Pearson Education.

Pantic, N. (2017). An exploratory study of teacher agency for social justice. *Teaching and Teacher Education*, *66*, 219–230. https://doi.org/10.1016/j.tate.2017.04.008

Philpott, C., & Oates, C. (2017). Teacher agency and professional learning communities: What can learning rounds in Scotland teach us? *Professional Development in Education, 43*(3), 318–333. https://doi.org/10.1080/19415257.2016.1180316

Pinar, W. F. (2012). *What is curriculum theory?* (2nd ed.). Routledge.

Quaglia Institute Voice & Aspirations. (2020). Voice definition. *A School Voice Brief.* www.quagliainstitute.org

Rosenholtz, S. (1991). *Teachers' workplace.* Teachers College Press.

Sarason, S. B. (1992). *The predictable failure of educational reform: Can we change course before it's too late?* Jossey-Bass.

Sehrawat, J. (2014). Teacher autonomy: Key to teaching success. *Bhartiyam International Journal of Education & Research, 4*(1), 1–8. ISSN:2277-1255.

Short, P. M. (1994). Defining teacher empowerment. *Education, 114*(4), 488–493. www.projectinnovation.biz/education_2006.html

Short, P. M., & Rinehart, J. S. (1992). School participant empowerment scale: Assessment of the level of empowerment within the school environment. *Educational and Psychological Measurement, 52*(4) 951–961. https://doi.org/10.1177/0013164492052004018

Strong, L. E. G., & Yoshida, R. K. (2014). Teachers' autonomy in today's educational climate: Current perceptions from an acceptable instrument. *Educational Studies, 50*(2), 123–145. https://doi.org/10.1080/00131946.2014.880922

Tao, J., & Gao, X. (2017). Teacher agency and identity commitment in curricular reform. *Teaching and Teacher Education, 63*, 346–355. https://doi.org/10.1016/j.tate.2017.01.010

Torres, A. C. (2014). Are we architects or construction workers? Re-examining teacher autonomy and turnover in charter schools. *Education Policy Analysis Archives, 22*(124). http://doi.org/10.14507/epaa.v22.1614

Trust, T. (2017). Motivation, empowerment, and innovation: Teachers' beliefs about how participating in the Edmodo math subject community shapes teaching and learning. *Journal of Research on Technology in Education, 49*(1–2), 16–30. https://doi.org/10.1080/15391523.2017.1291317

Tschannen-Moran, M. (2014). *Trust matters: Leadership for successful schools* (2nd ed.). Jossey-Bass.

Tschannen-Moran, M., & Barr, M. (2004). Fostering student learning: The relationship of collective teacher efficacy and student achievement. *Leadership and Policy in Schools, 3*(3), 189–209. https://doi.org/10.1080/15700760490503706

Tschannen-Moran, M., Woolfolk Hoy, A., & Hoy, W. K. (1998). Teacher efficacy: Its meaning and measure. *Review of Educational Research, 68*(2), 202–248. https://doi.org/10.3102/00346543068002202

View, J. L., & DeMulder, E. K. (2009). Teacher as artist, intellectual, and citizen: Using a critical framework in teacher professional development that empowers voice and transforms practice. *Democracy and Education, 18*(2), 33–39.

Wasley, P. A. (1991). String the chalk dust: Tales of three teachers in the midst of change. *Teachers College Record, 93*(1), 28–58. www.tcrecord.org

Yoo, J. H. (2016). The effect of professional development on teacher efficacy and teachers' self analysis of their efficacy change. *Journal of Teacher Education for Sustainability, 18*(1), 84–94. https://doi.org/10.1515/jtes-2016-0007

Zepeda, S. J. (2015). *Job-embedded professional development: Support, collaboration, and learning in schools*. Routledge.

Zepeda, S. J. (Ed.). (2018). *The Job-embedded nature of coaching: Lessons and insights for school leaders at all levels*. Rowman & Littlefield.

Zepeda, S. J. (2019). *Professional development: What works* (3rd ed.). Routledge.

Zepeda, S. J., & Lanoue, P. D. (2021). *K-12 school leaders navigate unknown futures: New narratives amid COVID-19*. Routledge.

Understanding and Framing School Culture

DOI: 10.4324/9781003222651-2

Examining School Culture

A low-performing high school was in search of a new principal to lead through challenging times marked by low performance, high teacher turn-over, and a climate and culture that was described as destitute and toxic. The principal hiring committee completed an extensive assessment of the leadership needs and wants from the school and community to identify the desired skill set for the new principal. The hiring committee analyzed the data from all groups and found quite interestingly that school culture emerged as the number one concern.

They determined that while the school was supplied with ample resources including the support of numerous instructional models, a wide range of classroom materials, and instructional coaches, the work in the classroom remained inconsistent and, in many cases, ineffective. Many of the comments from teachers blamed the previous principal for the working condition of the school and the main reason teachers left.

Although the committee wanted to focus on culture, they could not come to agreement on its definition or identify how leaders impact it. To this end, the hiring committee decided to engage in their own research to help them in developing the leader qualities they sought. The areas that the committee would examine included the:

1. differences between culture and climate; and,
2. internal and external factors that impact culture.

From this information, the search committee believed they would be better positioned in defining the qualities sought in their new principal that they wanted to create and lead a culture vision.

Introduction

School culture is the foundation that influences all human interactions within the system. The power of a healthy and vibrant school culture does not just "happen." Cultures are built through people in specific contexts influenced by internal and external factors that make a school unique. The ability of school leaders and teachers to understand and to leverage the power of culture and its subsequent relationship with school climate are essential to improve schools and the experiences students have in classrooms. This chapter unpacks the meanings of school culture and climate and examines internal and external factors that influence them.

Culture and Climate Differ

In fast paced environments, the challenge of understanding culture and climate is often compounded by misunderstanding the differences between them given the overlapping traits of each. Culture and climate are closely related, but there are nuanced differences between them. A distinction can be made by describing climate as the "attitude or mood" of the school and the culture as the "personality or values of the school" (Kane et al., 2016, pp. 1–2). Climate is perception-based, and culture is grounded in shared values and beliefs (Gruenert, 2008). In other words, climate is how people feel each day and can be more readily changed. Culture is rooted deep in the environment, involving the beliefs that make up the persona of the school.

In Chapter 1, the Framework for School Culture was presented pictorially as an iceberg that positions culture as the foundation from which climate evolves (see Figure 1.1.). Climate is the outwardly and more visible tip of the iceberg way above the water line that represents the sum total of culture while culture is the foundation. Within this foundation is a series of unifying elements that influence culture (e.g., teacher voice, agency, autonomy, etc.). As a pause point, climate is outward behaviors and actions; whereas, culture defines the ways in which teachers work together, collaborate, share, and take responsibility to support one another. Culture is the ethos of the school. Although there are overlapping features, Muhammad (2009) indicates that culture is "the way we do things around here," and climate is "the way we feel around here" (p. 19). Clarity comes by looking at definitions that amplify the meanings of school culture and climate.

Culture Defined

Peterson and Deal (1998) defined culture as the "underground stream of norms, values, beliefs, traditions, and rituals that . . . built up over time as people work together, solve problems, and confront challenges" (p. 28). Fullan (2015) positions that the beliefs and values of the school are the foundation for culture. Teachers and their experiences influence culture, and Kohl et al. (2013) explains that experiences include the:

- individual's perceptions of surroundings;
- different settings in which the individual participates (e.g., home, community);
- individual's relationships with others in these different settings; and finally;
- culture created by the interactions of the previous three levels.

Culture evolves through the patterns of actions and interactions from those within it. Culture is complex and dynamic because it is embedded within the context of a school, and this is why it is often difficult to define precisely.

In Chapter 1, teacher voice and agency were examined along with empowerment, autonomy, self-efficacy, and collective efficacy. These are some of the unifying elements found in Figure 1.1—all illustrating their relative relationship and complexity in the ways they interact to build culture. Later in Chapter 4, sense of belonging and an ethos of care make clearer the synergy that is built through these unifying elements. Examined in Chapter 3 are positive and toxic cultures. Culture shapes climate.

Climate Defined

As depicted in the iceberg (Figure 1.1) the indicators of climate are visible—people can see the tip of the iceberg. Climate "bubbles up" through the dynamics impacted by the culture. According to Cohen et al. (2009), climate reflects the quality and character of school life which is based on patterns of people's experiences that "reflects norms, goals, values, interpersonal relationships, teaching and learning practices, and organizational structures" (p. 182). These patterns are also embedded in the culture illustrating the overlapping relationship between culture and climate.

The National School Climate Center (2018) outlined key practices that support the development of a positive school climate which include 1) promotion of a shared vision, 2) policies and practices that promote the development of students, and 3) an environment where all stakeholders feel welcome, safe, and socially responsible.

Both culture and climate are important. The intersections between culture and climate are situated within a school context, and both are influenced by internal and external factors. At the heart of each are individual and collective experiences and the norms, values, and beliefs juxtaposed by school expectations and organizational structures.

Leading Culture

Understanding the Differences Between Culture and Climate

- Leaders must be able to identify and articulate the dynamics between school culture and climate and how such dynamics are both overlapping yet distinctly unique.

- School culture is below the surface of the iceberg defined by the shared values, relationships, and experiences of stakeholders. [see Figure 1.1. in Chapter 1]

- School climate is the outward representation (tip of the iceberg) of how the shared vision bubbles up through the dynamics of culture.

Leveraging the Power of Culture and Climate

- Briefly describe the culture and climate in your building.

- Based on the description of your school culture and climate, identify the dynamics that are currently influencing it.

- Create a conversation with faculty around their perceptions of culture and climate to determine if they align with your perceptions.

Internal Factors That Influence School Culture

Culture is created through ongoing events, conditions, and patterns of interaction found within the school. The internal factors that influence school culture are context specific and include teachers, workplace conditions, teacher morale, levels of engagement, teacher retention and attritions, and leader mobility. While there are many other internal factors, the ones presented here paint a broad picture of "life in schools."

Teachers

The research remains resolute that teachers have the greatest impact on student learning and that the environment and culture in which they work has a significant influence on their ability to impact student performance. Furthermore, in a positive school culture with high achievement, teachers have a strong focus on their students (Adeogun & Olisaemeka, 2011).

Although school culture is created over time, events can have a substantive and short-term impact on both school culture and the climate. For example, the conditions from COVID-19 turned the work of teaching and learning literally upside down. Teachers were in a constant state of flux; their patterns of working with students, families, and their colleagues continually changed. The importance of teacher voice and agency is paramount as schools experience an ever-changing environment (see Chapter 1). The work of teachers is central to student learning; therefore, it is essential for school leaders to support the development of workplace conditions where teachers can be effective especially during times of rapid change.

Workplace Conditions

The idea that teaching is a calling or a profession to give back resonates with most teachers; they are motivated intrinsically for reasons personal to their own experiences. However, intrinsic motivation is difficult to sustain when the workplace conditions erode the internal psyche to make a difference in the lives of children. According to Kamstra (2020), teacher motivation is impacted extrinsically by factors including workload, salary, lack of resources, a lack of social recognition, and curriculum limitations.

The OECD (2021) reports that "the quality of teaching and learning is determined not just by the quality of teachers, but also by the environment in which teachers work" and that "working conditions also play a crucial role for attracting teachers and for retaining effective teachers" (para. 1). Workplace conditions are embedded in the school environment and include, for example, daily schedules, rules, regulations, and politics. Often used interchangeably is the term, working conditions, that include, for example, workload (both in school and the expected preparation required off school hours), the types, frequency, and duration of support; class size; and patterns of communication and collaboration with other teachers and leaders.

Ladd (2011) found that school leadership is a "salient" predictor of working conditions and its relationship to teacher satisfaction and attrition is undeniable. Furthermore, Dean (2021) reports that leadership is "crucial" and impacts student achievement when they engage in:

1. Creating opportunities for effective teacher collaboration to explore student data, plan and review lessons and curricula, and plan and moderate assessments.
2. Involving teachers in whole school planning, decision-making and improvement.
3. Creating a culture of mutual trust, respect, enthusiasm in which communication is open and honest.
4. Building a sense of shared mission, with shared goals, clear priorities and high expectations of professional behaviors and of students' learning;.
5. Facilitating classroom safety and behavior, where disruption and bullying are very rare and teachers feel strongly supported by senior leaders in their efforts to maintain this classroom environment.

(para. 6)

Kraft and Papay (2014) paint a compelling picture that teachers whose workplace conditions are nestled in a positive school culture can increase the ability to improve student achievement. Central to creating and maintaining positive workplace conditions is teacher morale.

Teacher Morale

The harsh reality is that teacher morale has steadily declined in US schools (Senechal et al., 2016). Over the last several decades, the well-intended accountability movements regrettably have exacerbated teacher's sense of efficacy, leading to significant decreases in morale as decisions about teaching, learning, and the curriculum have moved from the classroom to policy arenas (Erichsen & Reynolds, 2020). These account-ability movements have caused teachers undue stress because practices associated with them often go counter to their beliefs about what's best for children (Wronowski & Urick, 2019). The COVID-19 pandemic further pushed teachers to new low points as a result of the stress from continuous change and uncertain futures (Will, 2021; Zepeda & Lanoue, 2021).

When low morale permeates throughout the school, it takes a toll not only on teachers, but also on the performance of students, and the support of their community. Teachers in schools with low morale exhibit:

- indifference toward others—collaboration is not the norm;
- cynicism toward students, parents, and other school personnel;
- low expectations for students;
- high teacher turnover rates;
- high degrees of stress; and,
- higher absenteeism rates that correlates to student absenteeism.

(Boyd et al., 2011; Kronholz, 2013; Markow & Pieters, 2012; Skaalvik & Skaalvik, 2011)

Developing positive school cultures requires leaders to both value teachers and include them in school planning and decision-making. Positive school cultures are further developed through teacher engagement.

Teacher Engagement

Teacher engagement is essential to build and sustain a positive and pro-fessional school culture and is necessary "to aid educators in committing to their growth and development . . . leading to a stronger in-school com-munity of more effective and engaged teachers" (Hanover Research, 2018, para. 11). When teachers are engaged, they feel valued as an integral part of the school and as such, leaders must respond in ways to support their work as the environment around them changes. Teacher Engagement is critical for leaders to create supporting workplace conditions.

However, when teachers are not engaged, they become dissatisfied with the profession and students suffer (Gallup, 2014). The prevalence of disengaged teachers, nearly 70% of K-12 teachers from a sample size of 7,200, is astounding as reported in data from a 2013 Gallup Poll, where:

- just over half (56%) are "not engaged"—meaning they may be satisfied with their jobs, but they are not emotionally connected to their workplaces and are unlikely to devote much discretionary effort to their work.

- about one in eight (13%) are "actively disengaged"—meaning they are dissatisfied with their workplaces and likely to be spreading negativity to their coworkers [and] to their work.

(p. 26)

The decline in teacher engagement as well as low morale leads to disenfranchisement and adds to the rapidly developing challenge of retaining teachers in the profession.

Teacher Retention and Attrition

It is difficult to engage in the work of culture in schools with high turnover and when teacher shortages loom. In fact, a less-productive culture is marked with higher-levels of teacher attrition. The national demand for teachers is outpacing supply, and the gap is projected to widen (Sutcher et al., 2016). The global COVID-19 pandemic is also projected to have a grim impact on teacher attrition (Burnette & Will, 2020). What Ingersoll (2003) referred to as the "revolving door" impacts culture at its very core. Instability "harms students, teachers, and the public education system as a whole. Lack of sufficient, qualified teachers and staff instability threaten students' ability to learn and reduce teachers' effectiveness" (Garcia & Weiss, 2019, p. 1).

Merely fixing the teacher supply will not solve the problem. Instead, school leaders must now look at the organizational culture and climate of schools that affects teacher retention. The shortage problem is two-fold, one of lack of supply, but also one of turnover, often referred to as attrition or loss. There are two types of teachers reported in turnover data—movers and leavers. Leavers are teachers who choose to leave the teaching profession and that number is growing with 44% of new teachers leaving the profession within the first five years (Ingersoll et al., 2021). Movers are teachers that change schools or accept non-teaching roles. At first glance this does not statistically impact the teaching force. However, whether a teacher leaves the profession altogether or moves to a different teaching location, it still creates a vacancy at the school level.

Certain schools tend to experience more turnover than others. High poverty schools and urban schools typically experience disruption in their cultures due to perennially higher rates of turnover (Djonko-Moore, 2016; Ingersoll et al., 2021; Papay et al., 2017). Also, teaching positions are not equally affected by shortages. Content areas such as science, mathematics, and special education are more likely to experience shortages (Ingersoll & Perda, 2010; Sutcher et al., 2016).

Leader Mobility

Just like the revolving door of teacher attrition, changes in school leadership impacts a school in very profound ways. Developing and maintaining leaders remains equally important as retaining effective teachers. Why? Effective leadership is critical in creating the culture and climate needed for teachers to do their very best work on behalf of students.

Principals are the second most important school-level factor associated with student achievement—right after teachers (Day et al., 2016; Leithwood et al., 2019). However, like teachers, principals are leaving the profession or changing schools at alarming rates resulting in a substantive impact on teachers and students. Studies have found that principal turnover can lead to higher teacher turnover, which in turn, is related to lower student achievement. Moving forward, this trend highlights the crucial role of effective leaders and a focus to strengthen leader development and support (Levin et al., 2020; Parylo & Zepeda, 2015).

Leading Culture

Understanding Internal Factors That Influence School Culture

- Teacher perception of school culture—with particular emphasis on workplace conditions, morale, engagement, retention, and attrition—has a significant impact on student achievement.

- The role of the principal in engaging their faculty impacts school culture is essential for teacher retention.

- The internal dynamics—defined by the actions, beliefs, voice, and agency of teachers and principals—will shape school culture and impact student achievement.

Leveraging Internal Factors to Improve School Culture

- Assess the teacher workplace conditions, morale, engagement, retention, and attrition in your school. What patterns emerged?

- How have these patterns in your school influenced (positive or negative) school culture and climate?

- Based on these patterns, identify key areas to address culture improvement in your building.

External Factors That Influence School Culture

Cultures continually evolve as a result of the impact by events, issues, and disruptions within and external to the school. Disruptions such as the COVID-19 pandemic, weather climate changes paralyzing city infrastructures, and legislative mandates are examples that can influence schools. Common events such as continuous patterns of hiring to fill teaching vacancies influence school culture. Although there are an infinite number of factors that can influence culture, examined here are poverty, shifting demographics, student mobility and attrition, and divisive political environments.

Poverty

The impact of poverty on student achievement has been at the center of policy reform for decades. Much evidence in public education points to a deficit model where the expectations for students in poverty were far different than most students from higher income families. Furthermore, students in poverty often experience lack of health care, inadequate nutrition, and limited access to early learning programs. The expectations and conditions for students in poverty to support their education emanates from a school's culture and program decisions. Although caution is offered, it is common for children of poverty to:

- attend public schools in economically impoverished neighborhoods (McCrary & Ross, 2016);
- experience overcrowding in buildings that are in decay (Azzi-Lessing, 2017);
- receive sub-par special education services (McKinney, 2014);
- be more at risk of being homeless (Uretsky & Stone, 2016); and,
- drop-out of school at a higher rate (Bauman & Cranney, 2020).

The toll of poverty on children and poverty in schools was exacerbated with the disruptions caused by COVID-19.

Although recent reform movements in education including the No Child Left Behind Act of 2002 had many flaws, at the center was the recognition that schools across the country typically had a culture and climate of low expectations for student subgroups including those in poverty. Historically, school cultures have embedded myths about students in poverty, and many of these myths still remain. Some commonly-held myths about those in poverty that continue to cloud education include:

- People are unmotivated and have weak work ethics.
- Parents are uninvolved in their children's learning, largely because they do not value education.
- People are linguistically deficient.
- People tend to abuse drugs and alcohol.

(Gorski, 2008, n.p.)

For schools, increased levels of poverty may be one of the most significant challenges especially when the culture of the school is toxic because it has not shifted to the realities of support needed to level the playing field. Important to note, that often when teachers cannot see their culture as one of different expectations, the students can. Adding to the challenges of poverty has been the continuous shifts in demographics.

Shifting Demographics

The United States continues to grow more diverse, and in 2020, white students no longer represent a majority of American children. The composition of students has changed. In 1995, less than one half of all students were enrolled in a diverse school district, moving to 75% in 2017. Furthermore, diverse districts, once concentrated in parts of the south, east, and west are now found across the country (Meckler & Rabinowitz, 2019).

Demographics shifts across the country have created major changes in the culture dynamics found in most schools. For example, race and ethnicity has shifted in the last 15 years reflecting changes found in schools. Figure 2.1 illustrates the shifts in enrollments by race.

Emerging and diverse populations bring a different set of family and cultural beliefs, presenting a new urgency to understand school culture. Shifts in school populations often create a disconnect between the culture of the past with the present, with both carrying implications for the culture of the future. Often tensions are created between those attached to a culture of the past, and leaders who are forward thinking and responsive to changing dynamics such as student demographics.

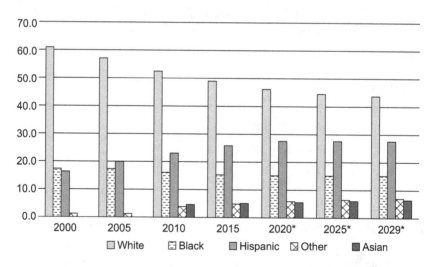

Figure 2.1 Percentage Distribution of Student Enrollment by Race—Public Elementary and Secondary Schools

Note: *Projected.

Source: U.S. Department of Education, National Center for Education Statistics (2020).

Another shift impacting culture is the influence of multiple languages spoken in a system, the emergence of English Language Learner (ELL) programs, and the types of services required by varied delivery models. Schools with high degrees of success with ELL students have reshaped their culture based on a new set of beliefs and expectations for their students.

Schools whose culture is based on predominantly white, English-speaking populations are less responsive to demographic shifts often creating resentment and resistance to change. In the long term, if the culture within schools is not recreated with the understanding of changing demographics, students will struggle, and any short-term change will have little long-term and sustained impact.

Student Mobility and Attrition

Changes in student enrollment continues as an issue as some schools have experienced a student annual turnover rate of over 70% before the COVID-19 pandemic. Typically, high student mobility is connected to low-income, immigrant and minority children, whose families experience rent instability resulting in frequent changes in housing and changes in the school they attend (Rennie Center for Educational Research & Policy, 2011). According to Herbers et al. (2013), the efforts of policy-makers and schools need to focus on school mobility to improve academic achievement especially with high-risk students and those impacted by poverty. While challenging at the elementary level, students changing schools at grades 6–12 need more focused attention given the greater challenges in social transitions. Today, the impact of poverty combined with Federal, state, and local policies have created divisive accountability cultures.

Divisive Political Environments

Community unrest along with divergent views on social matters continue to influence education. Today, movements such as Black Lives Matter, divergent political party positions, and federal and state mandates in education have changed the work of schools and the culture in which teachers and leaders work (Zepeda & Lanoue, 2021). For example, the No Child Left Behind Act of 2002 created what many view as a test culture, while the Every Student Succeeds Act of 2015 created a new political arena marked by greater flexibility for states to measure social-emotional learning and school culture and climate. Under ESSA, states are offered the latitude to establish indicators of student success that may include school culture. However, this national intervention for schools has created tensions and even divisiveness in school and research communities (Kostyo et al., 2018; The 74, n.d.).

The central question remains on who has the greatest influence on schools to develop cultures where students thrive and develop? Thomas (2012) proposes that public education needs to go back into the hands of the experts—educators. Public education needs a new political wall similar to the one separating church and state that no longer allows power brokers or corporate America to intrude on educational matters. Let policy be driven by teachers who understand the details and craft of teaching and educational leaders who are best prepared to do this work.

Leading Culture

Understanding External Factors That Influence School Culture

- Poverty impacts school culture; therefore, teachers and leaders must become reflective about how this dynamic impacts school-level interventions for children living in poverty.

- Student transitions, defined by mobility and attrition between schools and school districts, and shifting demographics impact school culture.

- School teachers and leaders have the opportunity and obligation to insulate children, learning, and school culture from divisive, external dynamics.

Leveraging Knowledge to Mitigate External Factors to Improve School Culture

- Identify the external factors that have had the greatest influence on your school culture.

- How do these factors influence school decisions, programs, and priorities?

- As a leader, how do you navigate the external factors inside the school house?

Chapter Summary

School culture and school climate share overlapping dynamics; however, each are distinctly unique in how they contribute to "school life." Leaders must be able to identify and proactively address culture and its relationship to climate. Both culture and climate are interconnected, and they evolve from systems of beliefs, experiences, and outcomes that empower teacher voice and agency. When leaders lump "culture and climate" as one singular construct, they fail to see the dynamic nature of the unifying elements under the tip of the iceberg. Failure to examine these unifying elements can create lost opportunities to develop teachers, workplace conditions, and fully support academic achievement.

Research shows that teachers have the greatest impact on student learning, and the culture in which teachers work has significant influence on their ability to impact student performance. Workplace conditions, teacher morale, teacher engagement, and teacher retention and attrition are the most important internal factors that contribute to school culture. After these teacher-specific dynamics, principal leadership is the second most important school-level factor associated with student achievement. To achieve the desired school culture, teachers and leaders must be able to collaboratively identify, measure, and respond to the internal teacher and leader factors that contribute to your school's iceberg.

Lastly, leaders and teachers both must acknowledge our schools do not exist in a bubble—external factors influence school culture. They have a collective responsibility to be aware of and responsive to the events, issues, and disruptions both inside and outside of the school house.

Leading Practices

1. *Analyzing* school culture and school climate in your school

    a. Find the intersections between culture and climate, what is the interplay between them?

2. *Developing Processes* to assess your school culture and climate

    a. Identify the most important internal and external variables contributing to your school's culture (below the surface) and climate (tip of the iceberg).

3. *Implementing Strategies* to leverage culture and climate

   a. With an understanding of the internal and external variables contributing to your school's culture, develop a process to jointly create strategies for improvement.

Suggested Readings

Gruenert, S., & Whitaker, T. (2017). *School culture recharged: Strategies to energize your staff and culture*. Association for Supervision and Curriculum Development.

Muhammad, A. (2018). *Transforming school culture: How to overcome staff division* (2nd ed.). Solution Tree.

Murphy, J. F., & Torre, D. (2014). *Creating productive cultures in schools for students, teachers, and parents*. Corwin Press.

Peterson, K. D., & Deal, T. E. (2016). *Shaping school culture* (3rd ed.). John Wiley & Sons.

References

The 74. (n.d.). *3 states cite school climate surveys in their ESSA plans. Why don't others use culture for accountability?* www.the74million.org/article/3-states-cite-school-climate-surveys-in-their-essa-plans-why-dont-others-use-culture-for-accountability/

Adeogun, A. A., & Olisaemeka, B. U. (2011). Influence of school climate on students' achievement and teachers' productivity for sustainable development. *US-China Education Review, 8*(4), 552–557. https://files.eric.ed.gov/fulltext/ED520461.pdf

Azzi-Lessing, L. (2017). *Behind from the start: How America's war on the poor is harming our most vulnerable children*. Oxford University Press.

Bauman, K., & Cranney, S. (2020). School enrollment in the United States: 2018. Population Characteristics. *United States Census Bureau*. www.census.gov/library/publications/2020/demo/P20-584.html

Boyd, D., Grossman, P., Ing, M., Lankford, H., Loeb, S., & Wyckoff, J. (2011). The influence of school administrators on teacher retention decisions. *American Educational Research Journal, 48*(2), 303–333. https://doi.org/10.3102/0002831210380788

Burnette II, D., & Will, M. (2020, July 14). Thousands of educators laid off already due to COVID-19, and more expected. *Education Week.* www.edweek.org/ew/articles/2020/07/14/thousands-of-teachers-laid-off-already-due.htm

Cohen, J., McCabe, L., Michelli, N. M., & Pickeral, T. (2009). School climate: Research, policy, practice, and teacher education. *Teachers College Record, 111*(1), 180–213. www.tcrecord.org

Day, C., Gu, Q., & Sammons, P. (2016). The impact of leadership on student outcomes: How successful school leaders use transformational and instructional strategies to make a difference. *Educational Administration Quarterly, 52*(2), 221–258. https://doi.org/10.1177/0013161X15616863

Dean, M. (2021). Our working paper on school culture and working conditions. *Teacher Development Trust.* https://tdtrust.org/2021/02/24/our-working-paper-on-school-culture-and-working-conditions/

Djonko-Moore, C. M. (2016). An exploration of teacher attrition and mobility in high poverty racially segregated schools. *Race Ethnicity and Education, 19*(5), 1063–1087. https://doi.org/10.1080/13613324.2015.1013458

Erichsen, K., & Reynolds, J. (2020). Public school accountability, workplace culture, and teacher morale. *Social Science Research, 85.* https://doi.org/10.1016/j.ssresearch.2019.102347

Every Student Succeeds Act, Public Law 114–95. (2015). www.congress.gov/114/plaws/publ95/PLAW-114publ95.pdf

Fullan, M. (2015). *The new meaning of educational change* (5th ed.). Teachers College Press.

Gallup. (2014). *State of America's schools: The path to winning again in education.* GALLUP.

Garcia, E., & Weiss, E. (2019). The teacher shortage is large and growing, and worse than we thought: The first report in 'The Perfect Storm in the Teacher Labor Market' series. *Economic Policy Institute.* https://files.eric.ed.gov/fulltext/ED598211.pdf

Gorski, P. (2008). The myth of the culture of poverty. *Educational Leadership, 65*(7), 32. www.ascd.org/publications/educational-leadership.aspx

Gruenert, S. (2008). School culture, school climate: They are not the same thing. *Principal*, 56–59. www.naesp.org/sites/default/files/resources/2/Principal/2008/M-Ap56.pdf

Hanover Research. (2018, October 3). *Five teacher engagement strategies to foster a collaborative culture*. www.hanoverresearch.com/insights-blog/five-teacher-engagement-strategies-collaborative-culture/

Herbers, J. E., Reynolds, A. J., & Chen, C. C. (2013). School mobility and developmental outcomes in young adulthood. *Development and Psychopathology*, *25*(2), 501–515. https://doi.org/10.1017/S0954579412001204

Ingersoll, R. M. (2003). The teacher shortage: Myth or reality? *Educational Horizons*, *81*(3), 146. www.jstor.org/stable/42926477

Ingersoll, R. M., Merrill, E., Stuckey, D., Collins, G., & Harrison, B. (2021). The demographic transformation of the teaching force in the United States. *Education Sciences*, *11*(5), 1–30. https://doi.org/10.3390/educsci11050234

Ingersoll, R. M., & Perda, D. (2010). Is the supply of mathematics and science teachers sufficient? *American Educational Research Journal*, *47*(3), 563–594. www.jstor.org/stable/40928347

Kamstra, L. S. G. (2020, November 13). Teacher motivation is vital—COVID-19 may be hurting it. *The Conversation*. https://theconversation.com/teacher-motivation-is-vital-and-covid-19-may-be-hurting-it-149345

Kane, L., Hoff, N., Cathcart, A., Heifner, A., Palmon, S., & Peterson, R. L. (2016, February). School climate & culture. *Strategy Brief*. Student Engagement Project, University of Nebraska-Lincoln and the Nebraska Department of Education. www.k12engagement.unl.edu/school-cli-mate-and-culture.

Kohl, D., Recchia, S., & Steffgen, G. (2013). Measuring school climate: An overview of measurement scales. *Educational Research*, *55*(4), 411–426. https://doi.org/10.1080/00131881.2013.844944

Kostyo, S., Cardichon, J., & Darling-Hammond, L. (2018). *Making ESSA's equity promise to close the opportunity gap*. Learning Policy Institute. https://learningpolicyinstitute.org/product/essa-equity-promise-report

Kraft, M. A., & Papay, J. P. (2014). Can professional environments in schools promote teacher development? Explaining heterogeneity in returns to teaching experience. *Educational Evaluation and Policy Analysis, 36*(4), 476–500. https://doi.org/10.3102%2F0162373713519496

Kronholz, J. (2013). No substitute for a teacher: Adults' absences shortchange students. *Education Next, 13*(2), 16–21. www.educationnext.org

Ladd, H. F. (2011). Teachers' perceptions of their working conditions: How predictive of planned and actual teacher movement? *Educational Evaluation and Policy Analysis, 33*(2), 235–261. https://doi.org/10.31 02%2F0162373711398128

Leithwood, K., Sun, J., & Schumacker, R. (2019). How school leadership influences student learning: A test of "The four paths model". *Educational Administration Quarterly, 56*(4), 570–599. https://doi. org/10.1177/0013161X19878772

Levin, S., Scott, C., Yang, M., Leung, M., & Bradley, K. (2020). Supporting a strong, stable principal workforce: What matters and what can be done. *Learning Policy Institute.* https://learningpolicyinstitute.org/ sites/default/files/product-files/NASSP_LPI_Supporting_Strong_Stable_ Principal_Workforce_BRIEF.pdf

Markow, D., & Pieters, A. (2012). The MetLife survey of the American teacher: Teachers, parents and the economy. *MetLife.* https://files.eric. ed.gov/fulltext/ED530021.pdf

McCrary, N. E., & Ross, E. W. (2016). *Working for social justice inside and outside the classroom: A community of students, teachers, researchers, and activists.* Peter Lang Publishing, Inc.

McKinney, S. (2014). The relationship of child poverty to school education. *Improving Schools, 17*(3), 203–216. https://doi.org/10.1177/ 1365480214553742

Meckler, L., & Rabinowitz, K. (2019). Six findings in the post analysis of diversity in school districts. *The Washington Post.* www.washington post.com/education/2019/09/12/six-findings-posts-analysis-diversity-school-districts/

Muhammad, A. (2009). *Transforming school culture: How to overcome staff division* (2nd ed.). Solution Tree Press.

National School Climate Center. (2018). *What is school climate and why is it important?* www.schoolclimate.org/school-climate

No Child Left Behind Act of 2002, Public Law PL 107–110. (2001). www2. ed.gov/policy/elsec/leg/esea02/107-110.pdf

OECD. (2021). *Review education policies: Teacher working conditions.* https://gpseducation.oecd.org/revieweducationpolicies/#!node=4173 4&filter=all

Papay, J. P., Bacher-Hicks, A., Page, L. C., & Marinell, W. H. (2017). The challenge of teacher retention in urban schools: Evidence of variation from a cross-site analysis. *Educational Researcher, 46*(8), 434–448. https://doi.org/10.3102/0013189X17735812

Parylo, O., & Zepeda, S. J. (2015). Connecting principal succession and professional learning: A cross-case analysis. *Journal of School Leadership, 25*(5), 940–968. https://doi.org/10.1177/105268461502500506

Peterson, K. D., & Deal, T. E. (1998). How leaders influence the culture of schools. *Educational leadership, 56*, 28–31. www.ascd.org/publications/educational-leadership.aspx

Rennie Center for Educational Research & Policy. (2011). *A revolving door: Challenges and solutions to educating mobile students: Executive summary.* www.issuelab.org/resources/5981/5981.pdf

Senechal, J., Sober, T., Hope, S., Johnson, T., Burkhalter, F., Castelow, T., Gilfillan, D., Jackson, K., Nabors, A., Neuman, P., Robinson, R., Sargeant, R., Stanford, S., & Varljen, D. (2016). Understanding teacher morale. *Metropolitan Educational Research Consortium.* https://scholarscompass.vcu.edu/merc_pubs/56/

Skaalvik, E. M., & Skaalvik, S. (2011). Teacher job satisfaction and motivation to leave the teaching profession: Relations with school context, feeling of belonging, and emotional exhaustion. *Teaching and Teacher Education, 27*(6), 1029–1038. https://doi.org/10.1016/j.tate.2011.04.001

Sutcher, L., Darling-Hammond, L., & Carver-Thomas, D. (2016). *A coming crisis in teaching? Teacher supply, demand, and shortages in the U.S. Learning Policy Institute.* https://files.eric.ed.gov/fulltext/ED606666.pdf

Thomas, P. L. (2012, April 26). Politics and education don't mix. *The Atlantic.* www.theatlantic.com/national/archive/2012/04/politics-and-education-dont-mix/256303/

Uretsky, M. C., & Stone, S. (2016). Factors associated with high school exam outcomes among homeless high school students. *Children and Schools, 38*(2), 91–98. https://doi.org/10.1093/cs/cdw007

U.S. Department of Education, National Center for Education. (2020). *Digest of education statistics*. https://nces.ed.gov/programs/digest/d20/tables/dt20_203.60.asp

Will, M. (2021, January 6). As teacher morale hits a new low, schools look for ways to give breaks, restoration. *EdWeek*. www.edweek.org/leadership/as-teacher-morale-hits-a-new-low-schools-look-for-ways-to-give-breaks-restoration/2021/01

Wronowski, M. L., & Urick, A. (2019). Examining the relationship of teacher perception of accountability and assessment policies on teacher turnover during NCLB. *Education Policy Analysis Archives, 27*(86). https://doi.org/10.14507/epaa.27.3858

Zepeda, S. J., & Lanoue, P. D. (2021). *K-12 school leaders navigate unknown futures: New narratives amid COVID-19*. Routledge.

Understanding Functional and Dysfunctional Cultures

DOI: 10.4324/9781003222651-3

Examining School Culture

One of the district school improvement goals for the upcoming year is for each school to focus on improving culture by assessing its health and developing an improvement plan. A new principal of one of the district's elementary schools had a proven record of school improvement by creating schools with supportive culture for teachers and developing effective improvement practices.

The principal's entry plan centered on assessing the school's culture to determine its level of functionality and unique attributes due to its history, traditions, and staff. After two months, the principal found pockets of excellent teaching and a general consensus that the school was doing an adequate job. However, it was also discovered that many of the teachers were overall disengaged, worked in isolation, and felt the school lacked direction and purpose.

The principal met with the faculty and discussed observations and shared perspectives about the value of school culture. The principal then used an activity to begin creating a picture of a positive culture that should exist in the school. The activity began by collectively identifying and listing the attributes of a positive culture. The principal then engaged the faculty in rank ordering these attributes. Once the faculty agreed on the attributes of a positive culture for their school, they then identified supportive school practices that were already present but could be further supported. The same activity was used to determine the attributes of a dysfunctional culture and the practices that currently existed in the school that could be modified.

The attributes and the supportive and non-supportive practices were given to the school improvement team. This team would draft a school improvement agenda using the information gathered from the all-school culture activity. The plan would then be vetted seeking whole-school input to ensure teachers were collectively involved.

Introduction

Understanding the dynamics and levels of functionality of culture is essential to creating schools that build the capacity to engage and educate all children. A positive school culture is foundational to support the work of teachers. A critical responsibility of leaders is to understand the characteristics of functional and dysfunctional school cultures. Culture is built by internal and external stakeholders; however, "principals communicate core values in their everyday work" (Peterson & Deal, 1998, p. 30). It is this work that situates the leader in the context of better understanding the complexity of the school's culture. To this end, principals become the "role models of the school culture" (Turan & Bektas, 2013, p. 162). This chapter examines leading a culture vision, characteristics of functional and dysfunctional cultures, and approaches to revisioning school culture.

Leading Through a Culture Vision

For school leaders, culture is not always on the forefront of their improvement efforts due to its invisible nature as compared to more tangible improvement strategies designed to meet the performance requirements of the State and Federal requirements (Lanoue, 2019). Leaders with a culture vision understand how it supports the needs of teachers and their readiness to make changes to improve. To deepen their understanding, leaders need to paint a picture of the culture that exists. In schools, the canvas in which the portrait is painted is not blank as every school has a culture which serves as a starting point.

When leaders fail to create a vision for school culture as they seek to make improvements, they may be able to make short term changes; however, these types of changes will likely fade away when the leader leaves the position. Leading with a culture vision and through a cultural lens brings about new insights and actions to improve schools for the long term. One may debate what comes first—culture or strategies and action—but in the end, culture is bedrock for lasting change for every school.

Understanding the Culture

The most pivotal role of principals today is to understand the dynamics of culture and how culture is influenced by the leaders and those within the system (McKinney et al., 2015). Shafer (2018) contends that "Once principals understand what constitutes culture—once they learn to see it not as a hazy mass of intangibles, but as something that can be pinpointed and designed—they can start to execute a cultural vision" (para. 4). Successful leaders must take a wide-angle view to deepen their understanding of their culture which in turn enables them to seek solutions to difficult problems. In challenging times marked by turbulence and uncertainty, the culture provides the basis of the enduring beliefs and values, which can be visible and invisible, and are related to the

- ways in which people respond;
- quality of decisions made;
- students, parents, and each other;
- ability to mobilize and innovate; and,
- beliefs about what is important.

The history of the school will unveil norms, beliefs, and attitudes that illustrate a school and its identity, what's important and why, the values embedded in behaviors, and points to the power-brokers—those who have had the biggest stake in the culture, or at least the way it was. It is in history that traditions, rituals, and stories tell a narrative of what the school and its teachers stand for—even if the narratives were built on a foundation that is no longer viable.

Leaders new to a school must first understand the culture and its history including the tacit assumptions, and the norms and conditions in which the present culture evolved. Regardless of tenure in a building, principals must always keep a pulse on the school culture. Without these understandings, the intentions of the leader can come into question.

Understanding culture takes time and requires a deliberate focus on the internal dynamics within schools. Observing teachers' attitudes in classrooms and during planning and other meetings as well as the attitudes of students toward their teachers is an important step in understanding the current dynamics that are the foundation of school culture (Raudys, 2018).

Through artifacts, leaders can gain an understanding of the school's traditions as well as the behaviors of those within the schools. Given that culture is embedded in the context of the school, it is important for school leaders to examine carefully the artifacts of the school culture such as routines and traditions and focus more intently on their meanings and the history associated with them. We all know that history is in many ways the sacred cow.

Culture Leaders

Creating and enacting a culture vision is about how leaders lead which is different from "what" they lead such as system improvement strategies. It is important for school leaders to understand their own leadership style and attributes as they conceptualize the existing culture within the context of the systems culture. Important for principals is reflecting about their leadership by asking themselves questions such as:

- Do teachers trust me?
- Do I support teachers as they make decisions?
- Am I consistent in the ways in which I respond to situations?
- Do I communicate often, sharing information?
- How do I communicate: by memo? Email? Face-to-face?
- Do structures promote collaboration?

The answer to these questions will provide powerful insights about the leadership needed to be a culture leader.

Also, critical for leaders is understanding their roles in supporting teacher voice, agency autonomy, empowerment, and engagement that are core factors that change and drive school culture over time (see Chapter 1). Leading a culture vision is not the leader's vision but rather a vision of those in the school. Kruse and Louis (2008) make clear

> Managing a school's culture is not dependent on the *authority* that you have based on your position, but can only be affected by increasing your *influence* over behaviors, beliefs, relationships, and other complex dynamics present in the school that are often unpredictable.
>
> (p. 1, emphasis in the original)

Developing a cultural vision is not about the strategies in place by the system but rather about behaviors within the system.

Leading culture is more than creating posters, slogans, and rules in that "culture is created through consistent and authentic behaviors" (Wong, 2020, para. 5). Culture is how you go about fulfilling your responsibilities and the behaviors you live every day which is different from strategies outlining what you want to accomplish (Richtsmeier, 2018). Principals who see change and school improvement through a culture lens embrace the power of the people within the system.

Leading With a Culture Lens

School leaders who see their organizations through a culture lens understand its impact on the work of teachers especially when aligned to the school vision. Referring back to the Framework for School Culture presented in Figure 1.1 in Chapter 1, the visible portion of the iceberg is what you see; however, below the surface is where the hard work of the leader presents itself. Leading through a cultural lens occurs in this space, the space you do not always visibly see.

Leaders must have a keen awareness of their role in leading culture and its power for improving the work of teachers and the achievement of students. O'Beirne (2019, para. 10) shares some baseline tips that have been adapted for school leaders:

- Understand if the culture you have can help meet objectives.
- Know the value of culture to your school, and the values that shape it.
- Understand how "tone from the top" is received and interpreted.
- Create confidence that your culture supports the reputation of the school.
- Understand how to influence the sub-cultures within your organization.
- Ensures the culture supports doing the right work.
- Enable a culture that promotes innovation.

Once leaders recognize the power of culture and their role in leading it, they need to understand the dynamics of functional and dysfunctional cultures.

Leading Culture

Understanding Leading a Culture Vision
- Leaders must be intentional about understanding how the history, traditions, artifacts, and attitudes contribute to a school's culture.

- To develop and lead a culture vision, focus on the "how" and the behavior of those in the organization—do not be distracted by the "what" and the strategies to be implemented.

- To understand functional and dysfunctional school cultures, leaders must adopt a culture lens that sees both visible and invisible dynamics.

Leveraging Leadership for a Culture Vision

- What action steps will you take to learn more about your school's history and traditions that influence school culture?

- Make a list of the visible and invisible dynamics that contribute positively and negatively to your school culture. What will you do with this information?

- As a leader, how do you discern between the "how" (behaviors) to avoid getting distracted by "what" (strategies)?

Functional Culture and Climate

Culture evolves in a context from the people whose experiences, values, and beliefs change over time. School culture is relational and is perpetuated through actions, customs, and rituals. Also, culture is influenced by internal and external factors, the experiences of those who inhabit the school as well as external influences that impact organizational policies, procedures, and structures (see Chapter 2).

Cultures are dynamic, continuously shifting and transforming as schools evolve to meet and adapt to the needs of the community and external mandates. Functional cultures require effective leadership—from both principals and teachers. Principals are effective culture leaders when they create opportunities for teachers to assume leadership roles outside of their classroom. Teacher leadership is necessary and created when they are able to exercise their voice and exert agency to act on their beliefs (see Chapter 1). Culture is foundational and influences every aspect of the school. Figure 1.1 shows that the Unifying Elements in the Framework for School Culture (e.g., autonomy, sense of belonging, etc.) do not sit in isolation. These unifying elements work off one another, influencing the ways in which people interact and treat one another. Culture encompasses the collective—good, bad, or indifferent.

There are many terms used to characterize a positive school culture and healthy climate as well as negative and toxic ones. Consider these terms that evoke an image about a school culture:

- Functional *or* dysfunctional?
- Positive *or* toxic?
- Productive *or* unproductive?

The terms used to describe culture should be understood by the community because teachers and leaders typically use their own language to characterize their culture, and more importantly, they live it every day.

Drilling back to Chapter 2, culture was framed as the "underground stream of norms, values, beliefs, traditions, and rituals that . . . built up over time as people work together, solve problems, and confront challenges" (Peterson & Deal, 1998, p. 28) with Fullan (2014) affirming that these values and beliefs are the foundation for culture. Peterson and Deal (2016) focus attention on collaborative working environments where teachers can freely engage in solving problems and confronting challenges.

Positive Culture and Climate

Positive work cultures unfold over time and are mediated by patterns that emanate from established norms that include, for example, collaboration and trust (examined later in this chapter). A school culture is ever changing as it is shaped based on internal and external factors examined in Chapter 2. In a positive culture, teacher self-efficacy broadens to a larger collective efficacy among community members.

First things first. Leaders are central to championing the school vision and its foundation of culture through their actions, decisions, and even their persona. All leaders, regardless of tenure at the site, need to understand the dynamics of their culture. It falls to leaders to be miners, sifting through patterns of interactions, school governance structures, teacher support in place, and how teachers and their work are arranged.

The dynamics of culture are complex and cannot be analyzed through a simple question such as, is the present culture positive or toxic? The answer to this question cannot be reduced to a "yes" or "no" response because culture is influenced by multiple factors interacting with each other over time. A culture can exhibit positive (healthy) and toxic traits (Peterson & Deal, 2016). Based on the image of the iceberg presented in Figure 1.1, unifying elements (under the tip of the iceberg) are nestled bounded by a foundation of teacher voice and agency. Table 3.1 examines often-found traits of positive and toxic school cultures that reflect the unifying elements.

The positive attributes of school culture and climate intersect.

Table 3.1 Positive and Toxic School Culture Traits

Positive School Culture Traits	Toxic School Culture Traits
Teachers are empowered—they have a voice and the agency to make decisions.	Teachers "follow" leaders.
Teachers feel a sense of belonging.	Teachers are alienated and feel isolated.
Teachers and leaders collaborate.	Teachers are controlled by excessive rules and top-down decisions.
Innovation is encouraged.	Teachers are discouraged from innovating.
Supportive feedback is the norm.	Feedback follows a one-size fits all pattern, and in writing vs. face-to-face.
Teachers feel supported, cared for, and safe.	Teachers are not supported in their endeavors.
Teachers are recognized for their expertise and have the autonomy to adjust teaching strategies, content, and assessments based on the needs of their students.	Teachers cannot deviate from board-approved curriculum and instructional strategies.
Teachers feel empowered to do their work and to make mistakes in a fault-free environment.	Fault-finding is the norm.
Teachers embrace collective responsibility to act based on their insights, deliberations, and beliefs.	Teachers are spectators paralyzed to act on their beliefs, expertise, and first-hand knowledge of the school and its students.

Positive Culture and Climate Intersect

Grissom et al. (2021) report that "a strong climate is one in which all individuals in the school can spend their time engaging in or supporting effective teaching and learning" (p. 64) where community members share common values, participate and contribute to decision-making, and support the aims of the school.

Positive school culture and climate is a precursor to teacher efficacy and better outcomes for students. In positive school cultures, teachers and leaders believe *all* students can learn and achieve. A positive school climate is created when the culture supports leaders and teachers jointly creating policies, processes, and practices to support student growth and development. In toxic cultures, teachers typically work in isolation and are often in conflict with leaders resulting in a climate engulfed in blaming each other for student failure.

Teacher development is central to a positive school culture and climate, and "teachers working in more supportive professional environments improve their effectiveness more over time than teachers working in less supportive contexts" (Kraft & Papay, 2014, p. 476). In Chapter 2, teacher morale and the impact of workplace conditions were explored while the power of teacher voice and agency were examined in Chapter 1. In a positive school culture, teachers are continuously engaged in professional learning with leaders empowering them to "be creative, take risks, find solutions, and do what needs to be done to help establish a positive climate in the school" (Combs et al., 2013, p. 124).

A leader's role in developing a positive school culture and climate is paramount—leader actions and interactions either promote or thwart its development, and effective principals "direct their energies to developing the group . . . creating a collective culture of efficacy" (Fullan, 2014, p. 55).

This deep dive under the hood of culture and climate illustrates that school culture is embedded within the beliefs and attitudes of teachers and their feelings of agency, sense of empowerment, autonomy, and self and collective efficacy (see Chapter 1). Moreover, positive school cultures are jointly led by principals and teachers who share a collective vision that serves to embody the ways in which teachers interact with each other, leaders, students, and other community members.

Critical to developing a positive school culture is understanding the role of norms and how they dictate the ways in which people interact and work with one another. In many ways, the norms determine whether a school culture and its climate are functional or dysfunctional and every-thing between these guideposts.

Key Norms Support Positive School Culture and Climate

Norms are unwritten rules of behavior that serve as a guide to the way people interact with one another (Chance, 2009). In their work, Saphier and King (1985) identified 12 key norms that, if present, would lead to a vibrant school culture (see Table 3.2).

Table 3.2 Norms That Support a Positive School Culture

Norms	Description
Collegiality	Teachers interact with one another in an open and straightforward manner.
Experimentation	Teachers engage in risk taking in fault-free environment.
High expectations	Teachers have high expectations for themselves, for each other, and for students.
Trust and confidence	Teachers trust one another, and they have confidence in their decisions.
Tangible support	Resources such as time and resources are available.
Reaching out to the knowledge base	Information is available to teachers so that decisions are grounded in the context of classrooms.
Appreciation and recognition	Teachers feel important, respected, and part of the school. They feel the work they accomplish is held in high esteem.
Caring, celebration, and humor	Teachers thrive when they feel emotionally supported. Communities celebrate—the big and small accomplishments of each other and students.
Involvement in decision making	Teachers are actively engaged in decision making.
Protection of what is important	Principals protect time and secure resources to support priorities.
Traditions	Traditions shape the culture and are upheld as part of the community.
Honest, open communication	Teachers engage in conversations about their practices in open spaces.

When norms are pervasively practiced within the school's culture, the ultimate outcome is what becomes most valuable—trust.

Trust is the heart of the matter, and Morel (2014) stipulates "Principals must work to create a climate of respect and trust. This does not happen overnight, and it starts with a positive example set by the leadership" (p. 38). Trust has been positioned as a "lubricant" that allows "more time to be spent on actions that contribute to organizational improvements" that supports a positive culture (Handford & Leithwood, 2013, p. 194).

Confidence is based on trust. Teachers must have confidence in their principals and without it, new teachers are more inclined to leave (Torres, 2016); teachers are not engaged in participatory decision-making, marking the school as an unhealthy one (Torres, 2016); and hope for establishing learning communities diminishes exponentially (Zepeda, 2019). Positive school culture and climate are built through mutual responsibility that leads to better school experiences. There is, however, a darker side—dysfunctional and toxic cultures.

Leading Culture

Understanding Functional Culture and Climate
- The difference between positive and toxic school culture and climate is identifiable. Leaders must be able to differentiate the traits of each to impact change.
- Culture and climate intersect through the actions of teachers, leaders, constituents, thereby contributing to the visible (above the surface) and invisible (below the surface) dynamics.
- Norms and behaviors that contribute to positive school culture are defined and practiced to contribute to higher levels of organizational trust.

Leveraging Functional Culture and Climate
- How can you identify, measure, and respond to the factors that contribute to positive and negative school cultures?
- In the same way we build successful schools around the premise that "all" students can learn, how do you ensure that "all" staff are engaged in your school's culture and climate?

- Identify the norms (spoken and unspoken) in your school that contribute to its culture. Develop a plan to identify which are positive and potentially negative and share this information with the school.

 # Dysfunctional School Cultures and Climates

Toxic cultures paralyze whereas in positive ones, teachers and others are empowered to act on behalf of the school and its students. Table 3.1 illustrated the sharp contrasts between positive and toxic school cultures.

Dynamics of Dysfunction

In general, a dysfunctional school culture is toxic "where the work, the atmosphere, the people, or any combination . . . causes severe disruptions" for the individual, school, or the community (Fuller, 2019, para. 1). In a dysfunctional culture, leadership is characterized as toxic, rife with double standards, inconsistent expectations, and checkered communication in which teachers feel intimidated to speak up and to exert agency. Essentially, teacher voice is squelched, and agency is supplanted with hyper top down and directive leadership where teachers and their workplace conditions are controlled.

Collegiality and Collaboration

Collegiality and collaboration are contrived according to Hargreaves (1994) who premised that in such cultures it is regulated by administrators, participation is compulsory, rule-oriented, fixed in space and time, and predictable. In other words, teachers are forced to engage by compliance. Typically, in such cultures, teachers do not have the agency to veer from the administrative script. As a result, Muhammad (2009) indicates that teachers have an "inability to properly respond to challenges and adversity" [and as a result], "educators in such a culture become stagnant, and their stagnation can be the catalyst for regression" (p. 83). In Chapter 5, collaboration is examined in detail.

It is unlikely that every aspect of a school culture is dysfunctional (or for that matter positive), and that is why principals and teachers need to examine the status of the school including, for example:

1. Structures and arrangements in which teachers and teaching are arranged.
2. Patterns of communication between teachers, leaders, students, and parents.
3. Beliefs about students—are they blamed for academic failure?
4. Policies—both internal and external—that hinder or encourage innovation.
5. Decision-making processes and their alignment to the school vision and mission.

The culture vision and the leadership to support it must drive efforts to reframe beliefs and attitudes; recast the roles that teachers assume; and examine the types of norms needed to focus on improvement. With an understanding of positive and negative aspects of school culture and climate, attention focuses on reculturing.

Leading Culture

Understanding the Characteristics of Dysfunctional Culture and Climate

1. Dysfunctional cultures and climates are defined by frequent disruptions and inconsistent expectations for stakeholders.
2. Leaders should assess the degree of dysfunction across a variety of indicators, including but not limited to patterns of communication, beliefs about students, policies, and decision-making processes.
3. The culture vision should seek to reframe attitudes that erode trust and create organizational dysfunction.

Leveraging the Power to Address Dysfunctional Culture and Climate

1. Identify specific dynamics in your school that undermine the positive school culture and climate you wish to establish?

2. From this list, engage the faculty in developing solutions to improve the undermining dynamics of your school's culture.

3. From this work, what priorities need to shift related to school structures, routines, and policies?

Changing the Culture Vision

While single actions or events by school leaders may have a modest impact on culture, substantive and long-lasting culture shifts require system processes. In addition, impacting culture is neither bottom up nor top down. Efforts to change the culture from the top down are often ineffective because they are viewed as someone else's project while bottom-up initiatives lack the buy-in and resources from leaders (Friday Pulse, n.d.). Beaudoin and Taylor (2015) assert that culture change needs a bi-directional and simultaneous approach where school leaders and teachers meet in the middle. Changing culture requires a delicate balance between top down and bottom-up approaches guided by the school's mission and shared beliefs.

Reculturing

Examining the dynamics of reculturing is a continuous process. Fullan (2019) magnified, "Reculturing is a contact sport that involves hard, labor-intensive work. It takes time and it never ends" (p. 42). While culture may appear relatively static, the dynamics occurring "under the tip of the iceberg" are in constant motion. Internal and external dynamics influence school culture, and people respond and behave in accordance with the norms, unwritten but tacitly understood ways of "doing things around here."

Internal and external events, policies, and practices influence the rate and pace of reculturing. For example, pre-No Child Left Behind, teachers had more latitude to make decisions about curriculum and assessment. Schools were motivated to change with national and state accountability standards and threats of sanctions combined with raising the expectations by identifying subgroup student performance. Some schools developed positive school cultures founded on closing achievement gaps using standards and formative assessments for learning. While other schools became dysfunctional by developing a test-preparation culture that encouraged some morally corrupt behaviors (e.g., bubbling in student test sheets). Reculturing can occur voluntarily or involuntarily. However, the school's culture lays the foundation based on norms, patterns of collaboration, and workplace conditions.

Already established, it is unlikely that all aspects of a culture are completely positive or toxic. It is realistic to assume that schools have both positive and toxic aspects embedded in their cultures. The challenge for school leaders is "changing behavior, of persuading people to act in new ways" (Eaker & Keating, 2008, p. 16). Reculturing involves examining beliefs, expectations, and assumptions to promote a collective sense of purpose (Fullan, 2016, 2019). Without awareness, it's hard to chip away at changing thinking, behaviors, and norms—positive or toxic—because they are embedded in school culture.

There are two types of change according to Maier (1987). First-order change is more directive-oriented, involving individual or small pockets of teachers, and does not change thinking or attitudes. First-order change is immediate and compliance-driven. Kramer (2017) indicates that

> First-order change is often reversible. It does not usually require new learning and is meant to tweak what already exists. It is often supported by research. But in most instances, these changes alone are not enough. Missing is a shift in the beliefs and philosophies that support the change.
>
> (para. 4)

Kramer (2017) continues that first-order change "lacks purpose behind the change" and resembles "a checklist" (para. 14).

Second-order change takes longer and includes a considerable investment of time and stakeholder engagement. Through second-order change, the principal works with the faculty and staff as a collective to unpack attitudes, beliefs, norms, and behaviors. Second-order change is planned and focused on very specific aspects of the culture (Levy, 1986), it is purposefully disruptive, and it "involves seeing the world in a different way,

Table 3.3 Difficulties Compounding Reculturing

•   Loss of control
•   Uncertainty about the unknown
•   Concerns about competence
•   Increased work
•   Secondary changes

Sources: Fullan (2016), Hargreaves and Fink (2006), Sarason (1996)

challenging assumptions, and working from a new and different worldview" (Coaching Leaders, n.d., para. 5).

Change is difficult, slow, and incremental. Some will embrace the work, and others will fight every step of the way. And others will be ambivalent (Fullan, 2016). Table 3.3 highlights why change associated with reculturing is difficult.

These fears are real; however, leaders can no longer be complacent about engaging in critical conversations leading to needed changes in school culture.

Leading the culture vision means challenging norms and behaviors that prevent teachers from accomplishing the work needed for students to succeed, professionals to grow, and all to contribute to school improvement efforts. Anything less than positive and productive must be addressed systemically.

Leading "Good" Disturbance

When there is a need, effective leaders purposefully disrupt behaviors that impede improvement efforts. Earlier in the chapter, leading with a culture lens was examined. Part of leading is disrupting patterns of behaviors, norms, and attitudes that darken the culture. Not addressing these culture busters signals ineffectiveness and allows the continuations of predictable patterns of dysfunction. With intentionality and a laser focus, here are some steps to consider.

- *Prioritize the Work*. Make the time to seize opportunities to articulate what is important, what is unacceptable, and why.
- *Create a sense of urgency*. Addressing unacceptable patterns in a school's culture must be addressed immediately. In their report on

change, the Minnesota Department of Education (2019) offers a few questions to frame urgency:

- Why is this change important and urgent?
- Can you share the rationale for change of this urgency and magnitude?
- How deeply is this understanding shared?
- How can you frame the change for your school community?
- What are the right questions to share with them, especially where there aren't easy answers?
- Have you set up the right structures to allow the school community to participate in answering these questions?

(p. 10)

- *Lead by modeling*. Model more acceptable behaviors (words and actions).
- *Stay the course*. Consistently work with teachers and other stakeholders to support efforts to build a stronger and more vibrant culture.

There are no simple ways to lead purposeful disturbance. Important for leaders is to create safe landings so the process does not go into a free fall. Safe landings can provide teachers comfort as the change process unfolds. For the work of leading school culture, the safe landing is to work stabilizing school culture.

Stabilizing School Culture

Schools are better positioned to respond to internal and external influences by understanding the value of a stable culture. According to Pulakos and Kaiser (2020), "organizational stability is what provides people with a sense of confidence, security, and optimism during times of disruptive change in the workplace, which, in turn, allows them to keep calm, act rationally, and adapt effectively as the situation evolves" (para. 2). Whether a school culture is stable or at some level of disturbance or dysfunction, the role of leaders remains critical in bringing ongoing stability especially in times of change as in the magnitude of COVID-19.

63

Engaging in stabilizing a culture during disruption or in planned change requires leaders to share their beliefs as well understand the embedded beliefs within the school. Often, culture change requires unlearning past beliefs while fostering responsibility to create new ones. A leader approach to stabilizing culture should include:

- Connecting culture to the school's mission, vision, and beliefs.

- Recognizing and communicating that everyone is involved and their voices are important.

- Engaging teachers and staff in every aspect of developing solutions regardless of years of experience in the school.

- Reinforcing the importance of ownership because we are "all in this together."

- Compromising appropriately through ongoing conversations that respect dissenting points-of-view.

- Structuring the time needed to address change.

Culture change starts with beliefs and is not a quick event but rather an ongoing and continuous process that needs constant attention and engagement by school leaders.

The attention required to maintain a stable culture is in many ways comparable to a mechanic's attention to a high-speed race car. The performance of the engine is determined by its sound and needs constant tuning. For school leaders, understanding the performance of their culture is determined through continuous conversations and ongoing collective action.

Leading Culture

Understanding Culture

- Reculturing involves leveraging first-order and second-order change to positively impact specific aspects of culture.

- Leaders must be mindful of how to intentionally disrupt patterns of behaviors, norms, and attitudes that prevent positive culture.

- Stability matters, as culture change is not quick and requires ongoing attention, continuous engagement, and consistency in expectations.

Leveraging the Power of Culture

- What fears exist in your building that slow down the progress of culture change (refer to Table 3.3 for examples of compounding dynamics)?

- List examples of existing strategies for first-order and second-order change—which are productive or counterproductive in your culture change process?

- Thinking about the magnitude of disruption, what key elements are necessary to stabilize culture amid first and second-order change?

 ## Chapter Summary

School culture is not a hazy mess of intangibles that magically appear in a school building subsequently impacting student achievement. Rather, culture is a methodical, intentional process of dynamics—functional and dysfunctional, positive and toxic—that evolve from the history, values, norms, and actions of the individuals in the school. Leaders have both the opportunity and the responsibility to recognize and to respond to such dynamics to leverage positive culture change.

The unifying elements of school culture may be seen or unseen, just like an iceberg; however, they are always felt by teachers. To achieve the desired levels of trust and confidence in school culture, leaders must consistently pay attention and engage to amplify teacher voice and agency. Unfortunately, the pace of "school life" often creates disruptions and challenges that make this degree of leadership intentionality difficult to sustain and even harder to stabilize. However, this is the challenge and responsibility of leading school culture.

Leading Practices

1. *Analyzing* functional and dysfunctional dynamics in your school culture

   a. After identifying the specific aspects of "school life" that positively contribute to school culture and, conversely, erode trust, confidence, and ultimately school culture, prioritize the most important aspects to address.

2. *Developing Processes* needed to improve your culture

   a. Initiate a process to engage teacher voices so they can enact agency to support focusing on the "how" not the "what" to improve school culture.

3. *Implementing Strategies* to stabilize culture

a. With the faculty, develop a plan including a timeline to address the areas of concern with the outcome of stabilizing the culture by eliminating disruptive elements.

Suggested Readings

Beaudoin, M., & Taylor, M. (2015). *Creating a positive school culture: How principals and teachers can solve problems together*. Skyhorse Publishing.

Fullan, M. (2019). *Leading in a culture of change* (2nd ed.). Jossey-Bass.

Lubelfeld, M., & Polyak, N. (2017). *The unlearning leader: Leading for tomorrow's schools today*. Rowman & Littlefield.

References

Beaudoin, M., & Taylor, M. (2015). *Creating a positive school culture: How principals and teachers can solve problems together*. Skyhorse Publishing.

Chance, P. L. (2009). *Introduction to educational leadership and organizational behavior: Theory into practice* (2nd ed.). Eye On Education.

Coaching Leaders. (n.d.). *First order and second order change: Understanding the difference*. https://coachingleaders.co.uk/first-order-change/

Combs, J., Edmonson, S., & Harris, S. (2013). *The trust factor: Strategies for school leaders*. Eye on Education.

Eaker, R., & Keating, J. (2008). A shift in school culture: Collective commitments focus on change that benefits student learning. *Journal* of Staff Development, 29(3), 14–17. https://learningforward.org/the-learning-professional/

Friday Pulse. (n.d.). Why workforce culture needs systems thinking. https://app.fridaypulse.com/en/help-center/improving-organizational-culture/why-workplace-culture-needs-systems-thinking

Fullan, M. (2014). The principal: Three keys to maximizing impact. Jossey-Bass.

Fullan, M. (2016). The new meaning of educational change (5th ed.). Routledge.

Fullan, M. (2019). Leading in a culture of change (2nd ed.). Jossey-Bass.

Fuller, K. (2019, March 15). How to recognize a toxic work environment and get out alive. Psychology Today. www.psychologytoday.com/us/blog/happiness-is-state-mind/201903/how-recognize-toxic-work-environment-and-get-out-alive

Grissom, J. A., Egalite, A. J., & Lindsay, C. A. (2021). How principals affect students and schools: A systematic synthesis of two decades of research. The Wallace Foundation. www.wallacefoundation.org/principalsynthesis.

Handford, V., & Leithwood, K. (2013). Why teachers trust school leaders. Journal of Educational Administration, 51(2), 194–212. https://doi.org/10.1108/09578231311304706

Hargreaves, A. (1994). Changing teachers, changing times: Teachers' work and culture in the postmodern age. Teachers College Press.

Hargreaves, A., & Fink, D. (2006). Sustainable leadership. Jossey-Bass.

Kraft, M. A., & Papay, J. P. (2014). Can professional environments in schools promote teacher development? Explaining heterogeneity in returns to teaching experience. Educational Evaluation and Policy Analysis, 36(4), 476–500. https://doi.org/10.3102/0162373713519496

Kramer, S. V. (2017). What kind of change leads to learning for ALL? Solution Tree. www.solutiontree.com/blog/second-order-change/

Kruse, S. D., & Louis, K. S. (2008). Building strong school cultures: A guide to leading change. Corwin Press.

Lanoue, P. (2019). School culture is more than how it feels when you walk through the school door. K12 Insight. www.k12insight.com/trusted/school-culture-lanoue/

Levy, A. (1986). Second-order planned change: Definition and conceptualization. *Organisational Dynamics, 15*(1). https://doi.org/10.1016/0090-2616(86)90022-7

Maier, H. W. (1987). *Developmental group care of children and youth: Concepts and practice*. Haworth.

McKinney, C. L., Labat, M. B., & Labat, C. A. (2015). Traits possessed by principals who transform school culture in national blue ribbon schools. *Academy of Educational Leadership Journal, 19*(1), 152–166. www.alliedacademies.org/affiliate-academies-ael.php

Minnesota Department of Education. (2019). *Change leadership: A guide for school leaders*. Minnesota Department of Education.

Morel, N. J. (2014). Setting the stage for collaboration: An essential skill for professional growth. *Delta Kappa Gamma Bulletin, 81*(1), 36–39. www.dkg.org/DKGMember/Publications/Journal/DKGMember/Publications/Bulletin-Journal.aspx?

Muhammad, A. (2009). *Transforming school culture: How to overcome staff division*. Solution Tree Press.

O'Beirne, N. (2019). The power of applying a cultural lens to your organization. *EY*. www.ey.com/en_ie/consulting/the-power-of-applying-a-cultural-lens-to-your-organisation

Peterson, K. D., & Deal, T. E. (1998). How leaders influence the culture of schools. *Educational Leadership, 56*(1), 28–30. www.ascd.org/publications/educational-leadership.aspx

Peterson, K. D., & Deal, T. E. (2016). *Shaping school culture* (3rd ed.). John Wiley & Sons.

Pulakos, E., & Kaiser, R. B. (2020). To build an agile team, commit to organizational stability. *Harvard Business Review*. https://hbr.org/2020/04/to-build-an-agile-team-commit-to-organizational-stability#:~:text=A%20foundation%20of%20organizational%20stability,effectively%20as%20the%20situation%20evolves.

Raudys, J. (2018). 11 real ways to build a positive school culture. *Prodigy*. www.prodigygame.com/in-en/blog/school-culture/#leadership

Richtsmeier, S. (2018). Simple steps to transform your culture vision into reality. *Tinypulse*. www.tinypulse.com/blog/simple-steps-to-transform-your-cultural-vision-into-reality

Saphier, J., & King, M. (1985). Good seeds grow in strong cultures. *Educational Leadership*, *42*(6), 67–74. www.ascd.org/publications/educational-leadership.aspx

Sarason, S. B. (1996). *Revisiting the culture of the school and the problem of change*. Teachers College Record.

Shafer, L. (2018). *What makes a good school culture?* Harvard Graduate School of Education. www.gse.harvard.edu/news/uk/18/07/what-makes-good-school-culture

Torres, A. C. (2016). The uncertainty of high expectations: How principals influence relational trust and teacher turnover in no excuses charter schools. *Journal of School Leadership*, *26*(1), 61–91. https://doi.org/10.1177/105268461602600103

Turan, S., & Bektas, F. (2013). The relationship between school culture and leadership practices. *Eurasian Journal of Educational Research*, *52*, 155–168. http://ejer.com.tr/en/

Wong, K. (2020, May 7). Organizational culture: Definition, importance, and development. *Achievers*. www.achievers.com/blog/organizational-culture-definition/

Zepeda, S. J. (2019). *Professional development: What works* (3rd ed.). Routledge.

Transforming School Culture Is a Human Endeavor

Examining School Culture

At the end of a challenging school year amplified by COVID-19, a middle school principal received unprecedented resignations of teachers representing over 30% of the entire faculty. In an effort to understand the

DOI: 10.4324/9781003222651-4

reason for such a significant departure and to determine what could be done in the future to ensure teachers stay, exit interviews were conducted with every teacher who resigned.

While the interviews were kept open ended, the principal held a focus on the social emotional aspect of teaching and the personal toll over the last year and its relationship to previous years. During the interviews of over 35 teachers, the principal ascertained various reasons for teachers leaving ranging from retirement, moving to a different school or school system, and leaving education altogether.

While teachers left for new job options, the principal also found common themes from every teacher interviewed. The responses from teachers albeit after a difficult year, all indicated that the current year only accelerated existing concerns. Overall, teachers indicated that teaching was

- hard and getting more challenging;
- time consuming leaving little time and energy for their own families;
- isolating creating a sense of emotional paralysis; and,
- dangerous, often fearing for their safety and health.

The principal embraced the need to create a culture to support the social emotional needs of teachers for the upcoming year. In moving forward, the principal decided to craft a very different back to school letter to faculty describing what was determined as a result of the interviews, outlining possible new directions to guide moving into the next school year.

Introduction

The power to transform school culture is linked to the ability for teachers to have a voice and the ability to act on it—agency. To exert agency, teachers need a safe, welcoming, and inclusive culture that embraces their individual and collective voices (see Chapter 1). While school culture is often described in various ways across schools, there are conditions that must support the working relationships between teachers and leaders. Ever present must be championing positive relationships and caring deeply about teachers and others who serve children, parents, and the community.

Examined in this chapter are the human sides of school culture including relationships, sense of belonging, and the structures embedded in the school that enable teachers and leaders to work collectively to do their very best work with students—and each other.

Relationships Matter

While much of the focus of schools has been on the wellbeing of students, there is a renewed need to focus on the health of teachers. The impact of COVID-19 has accelerated a growing urgency to understand and to respond to the social and emotional needs of teachers and the importance of relationships and connectedness. Leaders now need to shift their focus from the intense national and state reform agendas to assume new roles to address the growing social emotional needs of their teachers. New approaches are needed to provide care, to establish positive and supportive cultural norms, and to break the path of teacher isolation.

Care and Support

In moving through the COVID-19 pandemic, much was revealed about the needs of teachers. It took the pandemic to bring to light these needs as well as to create safe and secure environments where teachers and their emotional and physical wellbeing are addressed. As schools reopen their doors, teachers, students, and other personnel are reconnecting—many of whom have experienced loss, displacement from their homes, and economic insecurity—in person for the first time in over a year. To reconnect in more meaningful ways, schools must be prepared to be places of care and support.

Social emotional support in schools is now a priority for teachers given the stress, turmoil, and double-duty most of them experienced during the pandemic. Ofgang (2021) suggests that school leaders prioritize social emotional learning for adults when they accept its importance; make the work intentional; include everyone in the process, and inwardly reflect on efforts.

These principles are important in building support in schools especially given increasing risk of losing more teachers. There was always a looming teacher shortage, now exacerbated with fewer teachers enrolled in preparation programs and the aftereffect of COVID-19. According to research by the RAND Corporation, Steiner and Woo (2021) report of their sample, 25%

of the teachers indicated they were likely to leave their jobs by the end of the 2020–2021 school year, compared with 16% prior to the pandemic. These numbers illustrate that one in every four teachers will exit the profession.

Schools are significantly impacted when a generation of teachers exits the profession and a new generation enters. Those who helped to create the school's culture leave with new teachers entering who bring different backgrounds and ideologies that will have an impact. For this reason, understanding the dynamics of culture and its impact are critically important as school cultures must be built on the foundation of its teachers who are the culture bearers (see Chapter 1).

Teachers need to be affirmed and appreciated for their work. Affirmation without value is not a strong motivator unless it is nestled in a community whose culture embraces care for students, teachers, parents, and community members. Noddings's sustained work about care and its moral ethic brings to the forefront that caring is a reciprocal arrangement where people have concern and empathy for one another (1984, 2006). Caring leaders are introspective, and they learn *with* their teachers. As the lead learners, principals should show their vulnerabilities in public spaces and by doing so, they are modeling a powerful norm—care.

Leaders underscore the foundation of care by exhibiting behaviors and dispositions and beliefs and values when they engage in care as a moral and ethical stance by modeling, dialogue, practice, and confirmation—all central to Noddings' (2002) caring framework examined in Table 4.1.

Table 4.1 Relating Noddings Caring Framework to Leadership

Component	Leadership Practices
Modeling	Leaders demonstrate care, serving as role models for how to care for others.
Dialogue	Leaders engage in conversations. People learn more about each other through conversations that are reflective and deepened through mutual understanding.
Practice	Leaders not only model care, but they also provide opportunities for teachers to practice exhibiting care and concern with their colleagues.
Confirmation	Leaders bring out the best in their teachers; they confirm efforts and place value on them and their work.

Source: Adapted from Noddings (1996, 2002)

Leaders who model the attributes of care can go a long way in supporting teachers.

As teachers evolve through the profession, they need social emotional support. According to Transforming Education (2020), understanding the social emotional learning needs of teachers requires a different lens than those for students. Important for teachers is having the competencies to manage stress, to create safe and supportive classroom environments, and to recognize the overall wellbeing of their colleagues. Ultimately, leaders need to help teachers by creating supports that are deliberate, focused, and customized to the context of their schools and the overall characteristics of their teachers.

The individual stress of teachers and its impact on their wellbeing and effectiveness in working with their colleagues may be one of the most significant emerging needs in schools today. According to Greenberg et al. (2016)

- Forty-six percent of teachers report high daily stress, which compromises their health, sleep, quality of life, and teaching performance.
- When teachers are highly stressed, students show lower levels of both social adjustment and academic performance.
- Interventions on the organizational or individual level, or those that reach both, can help reduce teacher stress by changing the culture and approach to teaching.
- Programs for mentoring, workplace wellness, social emotional learning, and mindfulness are all proven to improve teacher wellbeing and student outcomes.

(p. 2)

Providing support, however, is more than putting in place programs.

To deeply impact the wellbeing of teachers, school leaders need to acknowledge the emotional stress teachers experience and to embrace a proactive role in providing support. From an organizational perspective, Gonser (2021) explains that

> Schools must invest in practice and power-sharing structures that allow for greater, more frequent communication and collaboration among peers who understand them—both to provide emotional support, and to allow for more collaborative planning to manage the workload and the stress.

(para. 4)

Moving forward with lessons learned through the social emotional strains caused by the COVID-19 pandemic, leaders should consider

- collecting data on teacher working conditions and links to well-being. State, district, and school leaders should keep in mind that teachers from different backgrounds might be affected differently by their working conditions. District leaders should work with teachers and school leaders to design and implement a variety of mental health and wellness supports;

- helping teachers access childcare, which could go a long way toward alleviating stress and promoting teacher retention; and

- developing collaboratively clear policies for remote teaching and considering adopting technology standards for remote equipment issued to teachers—such as laptops, cameras, and microphones—and provide necessary training to support remote teaching in the long term.

(Steiner & Woo, 2021)

Programmatically addressing teacher social emotional health requires a review of current school organizational structures, teacher expectations, and workloads to ensure care and support of teachers remains at the forefront. Program changes along with the unwritten rules or norms send messages about what is important and valued within the school's culture.

Normative Behaviors Send Explicit Messages

In Chapter 3, school norms, the unwritten rules of behavior, were examined. Several norms, if they are present, hold the care for teachers at the center of the work of leading schools and developing people (see Table 3.2). Like care, trust is a key norm. Positive school cultures are built on a foundation of trust through relationships that are dependent on time and effort. Leaders develop trust by building relationships through their actions, the ways they communicate, and the respect and honesty they exhibit when interacting with teachers.

Leaders play pivotal roles in developing the norms found within a school's culture. Their professional and personal behaviors and messages strongly influence school culture. These messages and behaviors can have either a positive or a negative impact. As an example, leaders who positively impact school improvement develop norms to promote a learning culture, and they do this by engaging *with* teachers to refine instructional practices and by promoting teacher development (Leo, 2015).

Leaders must reconcile tensions created by any disconnection between their own norms with the norms held within the school and the community especially if these norms are not compatible. Whose norms are more important and why? This question is important to address. Leaders need to be reflective about whether the culture reflects the collective norms of the community and if these norms contribute to a positive school culture. Moreover, leaders need to reconcile differences between their own norms especially if these norms are not presently held by the community. Shafer (2018) suggests that school leaders need to ask themselves these questions:

1. What fundamental beliefs do you want community members to hold about the work they do?

2. What do you want community members to value as being right or wrong, good or bad, just or unjust about the work they do?

3. What expectation should everyone have about the appropriate or desirable way of operating; what agreed upon rules should guide behavior?

4. What actions and attitudes do you expect to consistently observe?

5. What will be the tangible evidence of beliefs, assumptions, values, norms, and behaviors?

(para. 3)

Because norms are embedded within the context of the school, they are visible in the daily work of leaders and teachers. Important within the school's culture are norms supporting positive and caring relationships as schools can be very isolating places for adults to work and to learn.

The Lonely Road of Isolation

In many ways, teacher isolation is paradoxical. Teachers spend all day interacting with students in their classrooms; yet, they do not spend sustained time interacting with adults (Flinders, 1988; Webb, 2018). Reflective questions for leaders include:

- What do teachers experience through their workday?
- How do teachers connect with other adults given they are assigned to be in their classrooms with children, not adults, for a large part of the day?

The answers to these questions can portray a very concerning picture for teachers, and the structured ways in which isolation unfolds and is embedded in schools. In his classic work, Lortie (1975) described three different types of isolation:

- *Egg-crate isolation*: Given the "cellular organization" of schools, teachers are physically separated, and they spend their day without much contact with adults. In other words, teachers shut their classroom doors, often teaching bell-to-bell, with little time to engage with their peers.
- *Psychological isolation*: Psychological isolation is related to how teachers perceive the interactions they have with their peers.
- *Adaptive isolation*: The demands of teaching are in a constant state of flux. These demands cumulatively create conditions that can overwhelm teachers who are continually adapting practices and procedures—often in isolation given compressed schedules.

Although much has changed since 1975 and Lortie's portrayal of isolation, isolation continues to be pronounced and even exacerbated by events external to the school as in the COVID-19 pandemic. In positive school cultures, leaders and teachers understand the impact of isolation and create opportunities to collaborate. They reduce isolation built through organizational patterns, and they minimize psychological isolation by fostering workplace conditions where relationships and a sense of belonging flourishes.

We understand the importance of human interactions and relationships, but more importantly, we understand the negative impact as Webb (2018) describes about "the teacher who is isolated from the other is missing out on conversations that often bring colleagues together physically, spiritually, and emotionally" (para. 2). At the center of teacher isolation is the lack of relationships developed through formal and informal structures, processes, and policies at the site. As leaders engage in transformation efforts with a focus on school culture, strategically focusing on structures that can build relationships and reduce isolation is paramount.

The common reasons from teachers and leaders for not building relationships typically relate to time and energy. Often echoed is the sentiment that "I need to prepare for my classroom," or "I have to save my energy to do my best work with students," or "I can't add another thing because my teachers are too busy." While these reasons are legitimate, school leaders need to see beyond these sentiments by creating systems so teachers can engage with one another. Adult relationships in schools matter.

Minimizing teacher isolation first starts with the relationships between school leaders and teachers. Suggestions for school leaders to build strong relationships include:

1. Understanding the school's culture before making wholesale level changes knowing that what works in one school (their previous one) may not work in the current school. Start from the position that teachers are doing good work.
2. Tapping into the experience and expertise of veteran teachers as they are an asset to their school and the profession.
3. Creating conversations with teachers about possibilities and how they can better leverage their strengths and gain new knowledge.
4. Being visible and engaging in ways to strengthen your own skills as well as those for teachers.
5. Seeking input from teachers and strategically honoring their suggestions.

Relationships are at the center of what schools do. In positive school cultures, leaders understand how strong relationships are foundational to pressing forward affiliation and a sense of belonging.

Affiliation and Sense of Belonging

In schools with positive cultures, affiliation, and belonging—both strong motivators—support retention, reduce isolation, speak to the ethos of care and concern for each other, and promote collaboration (see Chapter 5).

People want to belong and be part of a group, and they are motivated often by affiliation—the need for positive working relationships (McClelland, 1990). Affiliation is about identifying and experiencing the motivation to belong. Mitchell and Sackney (2000) noted, "People are engaged in a search for place . . . companionship . . . identity and belonging" (p. 3). Positive school cultures are the places where teachers can grow and can be nurtured along their career paths.

Feeling a sense of belonging is an important need for all teachers, especially new teachers during the first years of teaching (Zepeda, 2018). Figure 4.1 illustrates Maslow's Hierarchy of Needs (1943). At the bottom of the pyramid are basic needs such as food, water, warmth, and rest. Immediately above these are safety needs including security.

The next two layers are psychological needs—belongingness and esteem needs. Positioned in the middle of the hierarchy, a sense of belonging or belongingness, is the need to feel connected to other people and to engage in relationships (Baumeister & Leary, 1995). When teachers feel they belong, they have a more focused sense of purpose (Lambert et al., 2013); an increased sense of efficacy (Skaalvik & Skaalvik, 2007); less likely to feel isolated (Kelly, 2001); and less likely

Figure 4.1 Maslow's Hierarchy of Needs.

Source: Adapted from McLeod (2020).

to experience burn-out and stress (Skaalvik & Skaalvik, 2016). A sense of belonging is important for teachers to:

- derive meaning from their work;
- increase commitment to the profession;
- feel part of the school and its community;
- grow and learn from their work;
- feel valued; and,
- continue to be motivated during stressful aspects of teaching.

  (Allen, 2009; Bjorklund et al., 2020; Huppert, 2017; Zepeda, 2018)

Positive school cultures embrace belongingness as an antidote to isolation. An integral part of promoting affiliation and belonging is through the structures that support collaboration.

Leading Culture

Understanding the Power of Relationships

- Effective leaders leverage the power of school culture to support the social emotional needs of teachers.
- Leaders who establish and maintain high levels of trust understand how their personal and professional behaviors positively or negatively contribute to the norms within their school culture.
- The dynamics of the school day, whereby teachers spend a majority of time working with students and little time interacting with their colleagues contributes to being physically and psychologically isolated.

Leveraging the Power of Relationships

- What school practices have been established to support teacher communication and collaboration necessary to minimize isolation?
- Identify the behaviors of school leader(s) that are observable by teachers and that positively or negatively contribute to norms and school culture.
- How do school leaders keep the pulse of their school's culture relative to care and belonging?

Collaborative Structures

Positive cultures are marked by professional collaboration where "teachers and administrators share their knowledge, contribute ideas, and develop plans for the purpose of achieving educational and organizational goals" (Leonard, 2002, p. 4). This section examines the structures to embed collaborative efforts. Collaboration is examined in Chapter 5.

The structures needed to build collaborative opportunities and support systems are not random. Building collaborative structures are deliberate, systematic, and based on the needs of the school. The collaborative structures in place are context-specific, and these structures evolve over time. This discussion is to give the reader a sample of common collaborative structures. The role of principals is to offer broad-based opportunities where teachers are empowered and engaged as the bearers of culture (see Chapter 1). Collaborative structures support the deprivatization of practice.

Making Practice Public

Collaborative structures enable practices to become public in ways that teachers can jointly work on the complexities of teaching. Table 4.2 provides critical questions for leaders to ask as they examine what programs exist and how teacher's workdays are arranged.

Table 4.2 Programs and Arrangements for Teachers

Programs for Teachers
• What types of professional programs are available to teachers?
• How many teachers participate in these programs?
• Are there programs (mentoring and induction) to assist early career teachers in acclimating to the school and their new professional roles?
• What types of leadership activities are available for teachers?
• How do you find out the types of programs teachers would like to see initiated?
Workday Arrangements
• Are teachers provided time during the day to observe each other teach and talk about what they learn from each other?
• Is there dedicated time for collaborative planning? Grade-level meetings? Department meetings?
• How many teachers are involved in formal and informal leadership activities?
• Who has been involved in developing collaborative arrangements?

Establishing collaborative structures requires leaders to create "shared spaces" where teachers have time and opportunity to discuss and address problems, challenges, and innovations in ways aligned to the mission of their school. Embedded in these structures must be the core norm of trust where teachers and teams have clarity in their roles, and they are given autonomy in their formation, function, and development. The construct of teacher leadership as a school-wide structure is examined.

Teacher Leadership

The work that teacher leaders do can have a profound effect on student learning, school improvement, and the overall ability of the school to build capacity. Teachers want and need opportunities to enlarge their sphere of influence beyond the boundaries of the classroom without necessarily leaving teaching for a formal administrative position. "When teachers act with this type of authority, they are empowered because their 'voices' are being acknowledged and, more importantly, *heard*" (Zepeda et al., 2003, p. 13, emphasis in the original). Teacher leadership is essential to build school culture to the extent that later in Chapter 6, it will be revisited as a way to build human and social capital.

Context matters on how teacher leadership is defined and enacted at the local level. Katzenmeyer and Moller (2009) share that in systems where the culture is positive, teacher leaders are able to "lead within and beyond the classroom; identify with and contribute to a community of teacher learners and leaders; influence others toward improved educational practice; and accept responsibility for achieving the outcomes of their leadership" (p. 6). Advancing teacher leadership occurs when principals:

1. Leverage teacher interests to expand opportunities for their growth.
2. Create opportunities for teachers to assume leadership.
3. Provide professional learning that supports career advancement opportunities.
4. Support teachers to become experts in their field(s).
5. Value their expertise.

Structures that support collaboration are essential to promote teachers working in different ways and carry many benefits to creating and sustaining teacher engagement. One arrangement is the professional learning community model.

Professional Learning Communities

A common collaborative structure is the learning community concept originating in the 1980s. Effective Professional Learning Communities (PLCs) are organized in ways for teachers to interact with each other to improve their effectiveness by accessing teacher expertise and experiences, engaging in purposeful professional learning, and providing safety nets for innovation. Although there are many different ways to structure learning communities, they "redefined how teachers could work collaboratively to inquire on the impact of their instructional practices" (Zepeda, 2017, p. 63). The enduring features of learning communities rest on:

- positive interactions that build synergy among members of the learning community;
- cyclical inquiry on practice;
- capacity building;
- focus on students;
- deprivatization of practice;
- shared leadership within the group; and,
- collaborative teams.

(DuFour & Eaker, 1998; DuFour et al., 2005)

Teaming is critical. In learning communities, teachers "engage in constructive dialogue, reflect on and improve instruction, and learn how to become more effective in the classroom to improve student learning" (Pirtle & Tobia, 2014, p. 1), and moreover, teachers "become both supports and resources for their peers" (Freidus et al., 2009, p. 186).

Online Learning Communities

In the current transitions in teaching to virtual spaces, teachers have the opportunity to expand their professional learning community beyond the school and their district. Online communities became the lifeline for teachers to be able to collaborate, plan, and help to ameliorate the isolation that occurred when schools shuttered during the COVID-19 pandemic (Zepeda & Lanoue, 2021). Digital tools and online spaces allow teachers to engage and

- support and extend face-to-face meetings;
- increase efficiency (reviewing student work samples);
- give feedback to draft formative assessments;
- store work to create a public source of knowledge and artifacts; and,
- blog about a common curricular issue to share ideas, reflect about student work, etc.

(Zepeda, 2015)

Online communities and networks have now become the norm whether teachers are working remotely or in school.

Collaborative planning has steadily evolved as a way for teachers to connect with one another in the spirit of improving student outcomes.

Collaborative Planning

Collaborative planning allows teachers to jointly plan, effectively implement, and assess instructional lessons with professional development embedded as part of the process. Furthermore, collaborative planning provides opportunities for teachers to discuss new practices and to modify existing ones, instilling confidence for experimentation and risk-taking. Collaborative planning by its design is empowering:

> By giving teachers a space to work together as designers, you're giving them a space to develop, test, reflect, and iterate on their work—a space to grow. When teachers go through a design process and emerge on the other side with a designer identity, they have a greater degree of agency in blurring the line between teacher and student, and in supporting each other as they rethink what learning can be in the 21st century.
>
> (Rufo-Tepper, 2014, para. 17)

Collaborative planning provides opportunities for teachers to grow in ways to support the achievement of all students.

Mentoring and Induction

Mentoring new teachers by experienced ones is critically important to provide the support needed for them to grow and stay in the profession. Schools across the country are challenged as they face staffing issues, both as a consequence of teachers leaving their schools and perennial teacher shortages, now exacerbated by COVID-19. In many ways, early career teachers who had their first year in the profession in 2020 amid the pandemic will essentially have a second, first year of teaching in the fall of 2021. Moving forward, creating new teacher mentoring programs will be a critical step to stem this trend which is reaching crisis levels.

Mentoring is a mainstay of induction efforts where more experienced teachers engage with early-career teachers in classroom observations, instructional conversations about practice, and learning more about the context and culture of the school. School leaders need to understand the value of mentoring and provide the structure, space, and time resources to support early-career teachers and their mentors to unpack the complexities of teaching by focusing "very clearly on the core business of education, that is, teaching and student learning" (Hudson, 2012, p. 81). Coaching, feedback, and reflection are ways to embed learning for early-career teachers, and Goldrick (2016) summarizes that "high quality induction programs can accelerate new teachers' professional growth, making them more effective and faster" (p. i).

Structures that support collaboration are essential to promote teachers working in different ways and carry many benefits to creating and sustaining teacher engagement focused on positive school cultures.

Leading Culture

Understanding Collaborative Structures
- Shared spaces where teachers jointly and publicly work on the practice of teaching helps to avoid the privatization that may naturally occur in schools.
- School leaders need to be intentional about developing, promoting, and nurturing opportunities for teachers to be leaders.
- A school culture built through teacher professional learning communities, which may include collaborative teacher teams, online communities, mentorships, and teacher induction programs is

critically important in redefining how teachers interact with one another.

Leveraging the Power of Collaborative Cultures

- What is in place for teachers to observe one another and to interact collaboratively with each other related to instructional practices?

- Describe the leadership opportunities in your school building that are open to all teachers and how these opportunities promote professional growth.

- Identify ways in which school leaders model their support for professional learning communities, teacher mentorship, and teacher induction.

 ## Chapter Summary

Schools are in the people business and relationships matter. Leaders must be intentional about developing a school culture in which teachers are affirmed and their social emotional needs are acknowledged and addressed. School norms should, in turn, reinforce those competencies that help manage the stress and isolationism experienced by teachers. Further, leaders should be reflective about how their personal and professional behavior sends explicit messages to staff that either builds or erodes the desired levels of trust. Teaching can be a lonely experience below the tip of the iceberg unless teachers feel affirmation and a sense of belonging to the school and one another.

There are many opportunities to establish collaborative structures and teacher support systems in the school. Teachers can be encouraged to jointly work on the complexity of teaching, whereby they are given the time and space to discuss the problems, challenges, and innovations in both their classrooms and, more broadly, their school. Additionally, teacher leadership opportunities—which do not need to be exclusively defined by leaving the classroom for a future administrative position—give voice and agency to those teachers who desire to expand their scope of influence within, between, and beyond the classroom.

Lastly, and perhaps most importantly, is when school leaders create such opportunities for teacher connectedness and empowerment. Not everything can occur before or after the school day or during the few minutes that exist between class changes and restroom breaks.

Leading Practices

1. *Analyzing* support and collaborative structures in your school
    a. List the opportunities that exist in your school for teachers to interact in ways that promote teacher well-being and nurture sustained professional collaboration.
2. *Developing Processes* needed to improve your culture
    a. Initiate a process (or review an existing one) that empowers teachers to connect, engage, and support their colleagues in meaningful professional practice.
3. *Implementing Strategies* to examine collaborative structures
    a. Engage in conversations with your faculty to determine the needed structures to support and sustain professional collaboration.

Suggested Readings

DeWitt, P. M. (2017). *Collaborative leadership: Six influences that matter most*. Corwin Press and Learning Forward.

Murphy, J. F., & Louis, K. S. (2018). *Positive school leadership: Building capacity and strengthening relationships*. Teachers College Press.

Ozenc, K., & Haga, M. (2019). *Rituals for work: 50 ways to create engagement, shared purpose, and a culture that can adapt to change*. Wiley.

References

Allen, J. (2009). *A sense of belonging: Sustaining and retaining new teachers*. Stenhouse Publishers.

Baumeister, R. F., & Leary, M. R. (1995). The need to belong: Desire for interpersonal attachments as a fundamental human motivation.

Psychological Bulletin, 117(3), 497–529. https://psycnet.apa.org/buy/1995-29052-001

Bjorklund, P., Jr., Daly, A. J., Ambrose, R., & van Es, A. (2020). Connections and capacity: An exploration of preservice teachers' sense of belonging, social networks, and self-efficacy in three teacher education programs. *AERA Open, 6*(1), 1–14. https://doi.org/10.1177/2332858420901496

DuFour, R., & Eaker, R. (1998). *Professional learning communities at work: Best practices for enhancing student achievement.* Solution Tree Press.

DuFour, R., Eaker, R., & DuFour, R. (Eds.). (2005). *On common ground: The power of professional learning communities.* Solution Tree Press.

Flinders, D. J. (1988). Teacher isolation and the new reform. *Journal of Curriculum and Supervision, 4*(1), 17–29. https://eric.ed.gov/?id=EJ378724

Freidus, H., Baker, C., Feldman, S., Hirsch, J., Stern, L., Sayres, B., Sgouros, C., & Wiles-Kettenmann, M. (2009). Insights into self-guided professional development: Teachers and teacher educators working together. *Studying Teacher Education, 5*(2), 183–194. https://doi.org/10.1080/17425960903306948

Goldrick, L. (2016). Support from the start. *New Teacher Center.* https://newteachercenter.org/wp-content/uploads/sites/3/2016CompleteReportStatePolicies.pdf

Gonser, S. (2021, February 5). Building a culture that respects teachers and reduces stress. *Edutopia.* www.edutopia.org/article/building-culture-respects-teachers-and-reduces-stress

Greenberg, M. T., Brown, J. L., & Abenavoli, R. M. (2016). *Teacher stress and health. Effects on teachers, students, and schools.* Edna Bennett Pierce Prevention Research Center, Pennsylvania State University and Robert Wood Johnson Foundation.

Hudson, P. (2012). How can schools support beginning teachers? A call for timely induction and mentoring for effective teaching. *Australian Journal of Teacher Education, 37*(7), 71–82. http://doi.org/10.14221/ajte.2012v37n7.1

Huppert, M. (2017). Employees share what gives them a sense of belonging at work. *Linkedin Talent Blog.* https://business.linkedin.com/talent-solutions/blog/company-culture/2017/employees-share-what-gives-them-a-sense-of-belonging-at-work

Katzenmeyer, M., & Moller, G. (2009). *Awakening the sleeping giant: Helping teachers develop as leaders* (3rd ed.). Corwin.

Kelly, K. M. (2001). Individual differences in reactions to rejection. In M. R. Leary (Ed.), *Interpersonal rejection* (pp. 291–315). Oxford University Press.

Lambert, N. M., Stillman, T. F., Hicks, J. A., Kamble, S., Baumeister, R. F., & Fincham, F. D. (2013). To belong is to matter: Sense of belonging enhances meaning in life. *Personality and Social Psychology Bulletin, 39*(11), 1418–1427. https://doi.org/10.1177/0146167213499186

Leo, U. (2015). Professional norms guiding school principals' pedagogical leadership. *International Journal of Educational Management, 29*(4), 461–476. https://doi.org/10.1108/IJEM-08-2014-0121

Leonard, L. J. (2002). Schools as professional communities: Addressing the collaborative challenge. *International Electronic Journal for Leadership in Learning, 6*(17), 1–13. https://journals.library.ualberta.ca/iejll/index.php/iejll/article/view/447/109

Lortie, D. C. (1975). *Schoolteacher: A sociological study*. University of Chicago Press.

Maslow, A. H. (1943). A theory of human motivation. *Psychological Review, 50*(4), 370–396. http://doi.org/10.1037/h0054346

McClelland, D. C. (1990). *Human motivation*. Cambridge University Press.

McLeod, S. (2020, March 20). Maslow's hierarchy of needs. *SimplyPsychology*. www.simplypsychology.org/maslow.html

Mitchell, C., & Sackney, L. (2000). *Profound improvement: Building capacity for a learning community*. Swets & Zeitlinger.

Noddings, N. (1984). *Caring*. University of California Press.

Noddings, N. (1996). The caring professional. In S. Gordon, P. Benner, & N. Noddings (Eds.), *Caregiving: Readings in knowledge, practice, ethics, and politics* (pp. 160–172). University of Pennsylvania Press.

Noddings, N. (2002). *Educating moral people: A caring alternative to character education*. Teachers College Press.

Noddings, N. (2006). Educational leaders as caring teachers. *School Leadership and Management, 26*(4), 339–345. https://doi.org/10.1080/13632430600886848

Ofgang, E. (2021, June 8). SEL for educators: 4 best practices. *Tech & Learning*. www.techlearning.com/how-to/sel-for-educators-4-best-practices

Pirtle, S. S., & Tobia, E. (2014). Implementing effective professional learning communities. *SEDL Insights*, *2*(3), 1–8. www.sedl.org

Rufo-Tepper, R. (2014, December 15). There's no I in teacher: 8 tips for collaborative planning. *Edutopia*. www.edutopia.org/blog/rules-of-thumb-collaborative-planning-rebecca-rufo-tepper

Shafer, L. (2018, September 9). Building a strong school culture. *Harvard Graduate School of Education*. www.gse.harvard.edu/news/uk/18/09/building-strong-school-culture

Skaalvik, E. M., & Skaalvik, S. (2007). Dimensions of teacher self-efficacy and relations with strain factors, perceived collective teacher efficacy, and teacher burnout. *Journal of Educational Psychology*, *99*(3), 611–625. https://doi.org/10.1037/0022-0663.99.3.611

Skaalvik, E. M., & Skaalvik, S. (2016). Teacher stress and teacher self-efficacy as predictors of engagement, emotional exhaustion, and motivation to leave the teaching profession. *Creative Education*, *7*(13), 1785–1799. https://doi.org/10.4236/ce.2016.713182

Steiner, E. D., & Woo, A. (2021). Job-related stress threatens the teacher supply. *RAND Corporation*. https://doi.org/10.7249/RRA1108-1

Transforming Education. (2020). *SEL for educators toolkit*. https://transformingeducation.org/resources/sel-for-educators-toolkit/ Retrieved July 27, 2021

Webb, D. (2018, January 11). Surrounded by kids, but still alone. *WeAreTeachers*. www.weareteachers.com/loneliness-of-teaching/

Zepeda, S. J. (2015). *Job-embedded professional development: Support, collaboration, and learning in schools*. Routledge.

Zepeda, S. J. (2017). *Instructional supervision: Applying tools and concepts* (4th ed.). Routledge.

Zepeda, S. J. (Ed.). (2018). *The Job-embedded nature of coaching: Lessons and insights for school leaders at all levels*. Rowman & Littlefield.

Zepeda, S. J., & Lanoue, P. D. (2021). *A leadership guide to navigating the unknown in education: New narratives amid COVID-19*. Routledge.

Zepeda, S. J., Mayers, R. S., & Benson, B. N. (2003). *The call to teacher leadership*. Routledge.

Professional Learning Cultures Grow People and Systems

Examining School Culture

In a fast-growing community, the school district was building new schools at a rapid pace. In preparing to build and open new schools, the priority for the district was to continue their focus on building professional learning cultures in every school. Teacher collaboration was foundational, and every school created structures and developed processes for teachers to have critical conversations about their instructional practices and to engage in professional learning embedded in the context of their work.

DOI: 10.4324/9781003222651-5

With the opening of a new middle school in the fall, the priority was to ensure teachers in this new school understood and embraced the spirit in which collaborative practices have developed by the district over time. The principal has been in the district for several years, and she was purposeful about the commitment of the system while interviewing faculty. The system committed one additional month of funding for all teachers and staff to work over the summer to prepare for the school opening in the fall.

The first task for the principal was to establish that collaboration was at the center of how the leadership team and teachers needed to work together as a collective. In preparing for her opening to the very first meeting of the teachers and staff, the principal understood the importance of developing "the right" messages and activities that would carry forward her commitment to developing a collaborative culture where learning was at the foundation of all their work. This was the same message shared during the interview process.

The messaging and activities for the month had to reinforce and model how conversations and professional learning would pave the path for developing a collaborative culture centering on growth and development moving into the school year.

Introduction

The professional culture in schools evolves from the beliefs, values, and habits of teachers created as they interact together to grow and to develop professionally. Developing a culture where teachers can grow and improve their effectiveness has been an ongoing priority as schools seek to improve teacher practices. The urgency is clear, "teacher professional learning is of increasing interest as one way to support the increasingly complex skills students need to learn in preparation for further education and work in the 21st century" (Darling-Hammond et al., 2017, p. V). Students need teachers who can bring clarity and navigate the complexities of teaching children (Sutton & Shouse, 2016).

While effective professional learning has been central to improving teacher and leader effectiveness, its importance, as well as delivery, has not always impacted practices (Calvert, 2016; Zepeda, 2019a). Creating a culture of professional engagement requires leaders to intentionally redirect efforts to support teachers as they embark on the complexities of teaching and engage in professional job-embedded learning supported through conversations and practices that nurture growth. This chapter unpacks collaboration and professional learning.

Collaboration

Teachers do their best work when they are given opportunities to work collaboratively with other teachers. Teachers working together are more effective and improve the learning experiences for students (Gates, 2018). However, school cultures continue to exist where teachers spend much of their day working in isolation. For leaders, creating a culture built on collaboration rather than one of isolation requires strategic design, implementation, and monitoring of processes that foster the professional interactions needed to improve instructional practices.

Bringing Clarity to Collaboration

Positive school cultures are built on the foundations of teacher voice and their agency to enact changes on behalf of students (see Chapter 1). For adults, learning is enhanced when collaborative structures are in place (see Chapter 4) and the arrangements that support teachers shape collaboration at the school. The norm of trust (see Chapter 3) impacts patterns of collaboration influencing the ways in which teachers engage in deep conversations about their instructional practices, develop curriculum and assessments, and use data to make informed decisions about teaching.

Albeit important, the concept of collaboration has been around for some time to the extent the term has been cast as "overused" and "overhyped" (ThoughtFarmer, 2021, para. 3). In Chapter 4, the structures in which collaboration unfolds, were examined. What collaboration looks and sounds like within and beyond these structures is examined more intently in this chapter. Broadly, for the purposes of this book, collaboration is defined as the ways in which teachers work together for the betterment of student outcomes, to refine classroom practices, and to create opportunities for teachers to learn from job-embedded professional learning. Collaboration at its best is both formal and informal and supported by the norms of trust and care in a school where relationships matter.

Although collaboration has been defined and operationalized in a variety of ways in schools, national findings from the American Teacher Panel indicated that "only 31 percent of teachers reported that they have sufficient time to collaborate with other teachers" (Johnston & Tsai, 2018, p. 1). The importance and time needed for collaboration cannot be a blind spot.

Although still evolving, the research strongly suggests that collaboration

- has a positive impact on student learning;
- supports the development of teacher expertise;
- promotes a sense of responsibility for students;
- is shaped and influenced by school culture;
- increases teacher self-efficacy;
- supports induction efforts and teacher retention; and,
- is shaped by the leadership of the principal in creating a community of learners.

(Darling-Hammond et al., 2017; Goddard et al., 2007; Goddard et al., 2010; Hargreaves, 2019; Johnston & Tsai, 2018; Mora-Ruano et al., 2019; Pugach et al., 2009; Ronfeldt et al., 2015)

Collaboration is dependent on leaders and teachers creating a learning culture where "Working with others can enhance creativity, improve reflection, increase respect for others, promote team celebration, and enhance self-efficacy" (Morel, 2014, p. 37).

Leading a Collaborative Learning Culture

The mindset of school leaders and teachers is at the core of creating a culture of collaboration and togetherness that schools need as they navigate the constantly changing learning landscape. Ultimately educating all children cannot be enacted alone in isolation. The evolution of collaborative cultures where teachers and leaders function in a place of trust remains not only a priority but also, now a requirement.

School leaders are at the center of creating a collaborative learning culture by how they enact their roles and the decisions they make to support teachers. While one of the most significant challenges for developing a collaborative culture is the time needed for teachers to interact with each other, providing time alone is not the solution. Collaborative cultures are created by how leaders engage, support, and empower teachers in making instructional decisions. Furthermore, leaders themselves must be able to practice and model the attributes of shared leadership within the instructional space.

As leaders self-reflect about their own leadership attributes, asking key questions as presented in Table 5.1 sheds perspectives related to collaboration.

The influences of school leadership on culture is impactful. Leaders will have incredible difficulty in creating positive cultures if their actions and attitudes do not align to the school culture attributes they seek.

Table 5.1 Self-Reflection about Shared Leadership

Leadership Attributes	Key Reflective Questions
Collaborative Decision-Making	Do I just render decisions? **or** Do I support, encourage, and provide critical information for the team to make decisions?
Problem Solving Skills	Do I delegate critical problems to others and hold them accountable? **or** Do I include others in solving problems and taking ownership for the solution's success or not?
New Ideas	Do I see new ideas explored and accepted based on my thinking? **or** Are new ideas explored and accepted regardless of origin?
Professional Learning	Do I expect that all are professional and should be able to complete the expected work? **or** Do I assess my own knowledge and that of others to support the development of new skills?
Conflict Management	Do I get frustrated when people do not agree and want to cast blame? **or** Do I see conflict as an opportunity to bring people together in ways to see multiple perspectives?

Adapted from O'Neil (2018).

Leaders must ensure that their beliefs and actions align. Teachers will spot the inconsistencies when leader beliefs are not carried through by action. To build a positive culture, leaders must model expected behaviors such as care (see Chapter 3); they must empower teachers to exert their voice and signal confidence in their agency to make decisions (see Chapter 1). When leaders model collaboration, they send strong messages that the collective work of all teachers is what will make a difference for students. Collaborative cultures reflect a unique balance between a leader's responsibility to ensure the right work and the coherence of the systems with the autonomy teachers need to make ground-level decisions about best practices in the classroom.

Building trust and establishing relationships are foundational in developing a culture of collaboration. These processes mature over time as teachers grow in their confidence to take calculated risks through experimentation as they engage in increasingly more complex work with students. When teachers collaborate, they expose their vulnerabilities as they ask questions, seek support from a colleague, or share the results of their efforts. They need support, encouragement, and safe landings in taking risks with new instructional designs. Leaders support collaboration when they encourage innovation and when they provide safety-nets for teachers to engage with one another.

Collaboration is context specific and requires the acknowledgement of unique nuances given the diverse nature of schools, the systems, and the communities that are served. All of these ideas point to the need for creating collaborative cultures that develop from a primary focus of continuous learning for students, teachers, and leaders.

Creating a Collaborative Learning Culture

While teacher collaboration on the surface may appear commonplace among schools, the realities reflect significant differences in the opportunities available for collaboration, the frequency of collaborative activities, and its overall value to teachers (Johnston & Tsai, 2018). Furthermore, while different positions on what comes first: the belief in the power of collaboration and collaborative practices or the practices of collaboration changing beliefs can be debated, the reality is that they both matter.

Leaders will need to move forward in the context that best works for them and their school.

Creating a learning culture takes time and requires intentionality. Critically important is for leaders to

1. Make a commitment to effective collaboration processes as a priority.

2. Articulate the power of collaboration within the context of the school's mission, vision, and beliefs.

3. Provide opportunities for discussion related to current and needed collaborative practices.

4. Schedule adequate time for teachers to meet.

5. Embed professional learning during the day to support teacher effectiveness.

6. Allow teachers to be creative in how they work together.

7. Encourage teachers and teams to establish norms needed to foster collaboration.

Developing a culture of collaboration is not a random process nor is it always organic, percolating from the bottom up. Leaders play a critical role as they lead by creating the conditions that signal the importance of collaboration, its design, and how it supports the work of teachers.

According to Psunder (2009) "aspirations to establish a collaborative culture in schools first requires an awareness of the importance and necessity of mutual cooperation" (p. 2). Breaking years of teachers working in isolation and often in environments where individual practice was often protected, requires leaders to understand the current conditions and history of collaboration in their school. This history is important to engage in change leadership and the lens needed to understand school culture (see Chapter 3).

Because collaboration is built on trust and other norms, it is important to look at conflict that may arise while trying to create a collaborative culture (see Chapter 3). Conflict arises when entrenched norms and structures such as privacy are challenged and made more difficult by independent mindsets embedded in behaviors stemming from mistrust, defensiveness, and secrecy to individual power plays (Stanhope, 2020). Leaders must be attuned to these systemic challenges with the understanding that the culture and its norms change over time. These changes within a culture cannot be viewed as events that can be addressed and corrected in the short term.

Creating a healthy school culture cannot be accomplished by edict or top-down directives and programs. Leaders must engender in teachers a sense of ownership and model the importance of collaboration to support their efforts to be effective in the classroom. Leaders hold the responsibility to create the conditions for ownership and a sense of pride to evolve. However, principals cannot expect to harness the power of collaboration by simply putting teams together. Rather, principals must be clear about expectations, set the parameters, and ensure needed support is provided (DuFour, 2006).

At the center of collaborative models is how teachers engage in conversations that assess current practices, leading to new ones that better meet the diverse learning needs of students. Creating opportunities for professional conversations allows teachers to engage not only in embedded professional learning that is timely, ongoing, and specific to individual teacher needs but also supports the development of a culture built on collaborative efforts.

Leading Culture

Understanding Collaborative Cultures

1. Teacher collaboration is defined as ways in which they work together to improve student outcomes, refine classroom practices, and create opportunities for job-embedded professional learning.

2. Collaborative cultures are created when leaders engage, support, and empower teachers to make instructional decisions.

3. Leaders must create conditions that signal the importance of collaboration and how it supports the work of teachers.

Leveraging the Power of Collaborative Cultures

1. How can school leaders create and protect time for quality teacher collaboration?

2. Identify ways to nurture the trusting relationships necessary for teachers to be vulnerable during teacher collaboration.

3. What strategies can leaders use to create conditions for trust that proactively and strategically address tendencies for teachers to isolate and retreat to privacy?

 # Professional Learning

Throughout this book, voice and agency have centered on the need for teachers to be the culture makers of the school (see Chapter 1, especially). At the heart of agency is active decision making, a critical component of professional development (Calvert, 2016; Zepeda, 2019a, 2019b). Teachers want to learn and to grow as they move throughout their careers, and they want their efforts to result in increased learning for students, themselves, and their colleagues (Zepeda, 2019b). In Chapter 4, the structures of programs for teachers were examined. This section examines what happens inside these structures that support teacher collaboration.

Teachers grow and thrive in environments where collaboration is the norm. When teachers are empowered to chart their own professional growth, learning is situated in the very work they are doing in their classrooms and when they are collaborating with their peers. Schools and systems spend countless dollars on professional learning. This money is well spent only when professional learning supports teachers in their efforts to teach students.

Unpacking Professional Learning

For professional learning to sustain long-term momentum to support a positive school culture, leaders and teachers must be at the forefront of efforts to create the conditions such as the norms, values, and collective efficacy to lead learning for adults. Although teacher learning is a highly personal endeavor, "Teachers and school leaders share responsibility not only for their own professional learning but [also for] the learning of other teachers" (Jensen et al., 2016). The research is clear that highly effective professional learning is a collaborative process. Distilling 40 years of research,

Darling-Hammond et al. (2017) teased out the most salient features about professional development as presented in Table 5.2.

An essential feature of professional development is coherence. Coherence is developed by creating multiple opportunities for teachers to address their knowledge and beliefs through collective participation in the work required to be effective in the classroom (Desimone, 2009, 2011; Desimone & Garet, 2015).

To realize coherence, professional learning must "support sustained professional communication among teachers who are working to reform their teaching in similar ways" (Desimone, 2011, p. 65). In other words, everyone is on the same page connecting strategies and processes related

Table 5.2 Salient Features of Professional Learning

Features of Effective Professional Learning	*Description*
Explicitly geared toward discipline-specific content	Effective professional development is context specific, content focused, and job embedded in the realities of teaching.
Applies active learning strategies	To support teachers' learning, professional development provides teachers with learning experiences that promote engagement through opportunities for collaboration, coaching, feedback, reflection, and modeling.
Encourages collaboration between professionals	There is a balance between learning opportunities at the site with peers and with professionals outside of the school.
Models effective practice	Impactful professional development includes modeling and application of effective practice. Through embedding modeling as part of professional learning, teachers gain a deeper understanding of what effective instruction looks and sounds like in practice.
Includes coaching and expert support from a variety of sources	Professional development is enhanced through coaching and other support structures. These types of support provide teachers with guidance as they refine existing practices and adapt new ones.

Features of Effective Professional Learning	Description
Feedback and reflection	Learning is enhanced through feedback and opportunities to reflect about practices. Teachers make better sense of instruction and the types of changes needed to support the refinement of practice.
Sustained duration and intensity	The "one and done" professional development offered "here and there" is not effective and does not afford for cumulative learning. Effective professional learning is sustained and provides teachers with multiple opportunities to learn through a variety of modalities that support adult learning.

Source: Adapted from Darling-Hammond et al. (2017)

to the content and purposes of professional learning. Growth is more assured when it is situated in the daily work of teaching, which is referred to as professional job-embedded learning.

Focusing on Professional Job-Embedded Learning

Professional job-embedded learning, when situated in the work of teaching, supports collaboration, joint problem-posing, and problem-solving (Zepeda, 2019b). Furthermore, the underlying constructs of job-embedded learning promote self-efficacy (Derrington & Angelle, 2013); teacher agency (Calvert, 2016); and collaboration (Darling-Hammond & Richardson, 2009). These underlying constructs are presented in Figure 1.1 as unifying elements that when functional support a positive school culture.

Calvert (2016) confirms that teachers need and want personalized professional development and that "Teachers are in it for autonomy and mastery. They want to master their craft and be free to innovate" (p. 14). To create opportunities for teachers to be creative and to gain mastery, professional learning must be embedded within their daily work. The power of job-embedded learning is that it leads "to improvements in practice from the lessons learned on the job from teaching and interacting with peers" (Zepeda, 2015, p. 54). Learning is embedded when it:

- holds relevance for the adult learner—Adults want to derive value from their learning. Job-embedded learning is highly individualized.

- includes feedback as part of the process—Job-embedded learning includes feedback and collaborative support with built-in processes such as peer coaching after a team meeting or classroom observation. The feedback is focused on a particular aspect of the classroom.

- supports inquiry and reflection—Job-embedded learning promotes thinking more critically and reflectively about practice at the individual or group level with peers.

- facilitates the transfer of new skills into practice—Job-embedded learning provides ongoing support to help focus on the transfer of skills into practice.

- promotes collaboration—It is through collaboration that teachers share with one another, engage in discussions, and reflect about their experiences.

- situates learning in virtual spaces—The emergence of digital learning environments, platforms, and applications have connected the world by broadband width that allows teachers to communicate through Skype, Twitter, or Zoom, etc. There are infinite tools to collaborate with peers at the school site and beyond.

(Zepeda, 2015, pp. 35–38)

Recently, virtual learning spaces became the norm for teachers as they pivoted to online learning for students during COVID-19 and at present, the Delta variant (see Chapter 7).

A culture is marked by the types of professional learning offered to support teacher growth and development. It is important to understand that professional job-embedded learning is a long-term strategy that fosters a sense of responsibility to improve teaching practices (Hargreaves & O'Connor, 2017; de Jong et al., 2019). Short-term approaches predicated on quick-fix solutions will yield few gains for teachers and their students; moreover, these approaches will not sustain efforts to build a healthy school culture.

In a positive school culture, supportive collaborative practices are the mainstay of teacher development because these practices go beyond building individual capacity in that they support building social capital (see Chapter 6).

Promoting Supportive Collaborative Practices

The movement of schools as collaborative places to teach has created new opportunities for teachers to learn from each other. Whether new teachers interact with experienced teachers to learn from their practices or experienced teachers gain a fresh perspective from beginning teachers, the overall interactions and social connection serves as a reservoir of wealth for all. Leaders play a critical role by modeling collaborative practices, supporting the development of norms to define the ways in which teachers interact with one another, and promoting risk-taking to engage in conversations that unpack instructional practices required to improve student achievement.

Supportive collaborative practices embedded into the teacher's workday require structures to be in place (see Chapter 4). Models built on the principles of job-embedded learning include, for example, action research, peer coaching, and lesson study. These models are outside the focus of this book; however, they all have collaborative processes embedded in them.

As a starting point, teachers need time and space to engage in these processes, and leaders must ensure that they protect time during the school-day. Next, these processes in many ways overlap with one another. For example, after a peer observes a colleague, they meet to discuss an aspect of the lesson guided by classroom observation notes. During the conversation, the observed teacher reflects out loud about calling patterns while the peer coach asks open-ended questions to help make sense of not only calling patterns but also the differences between student responses when higher and lower-order questions were asked. During the conversation, the peer coach then models different question stems that would evoke different levels of response from students.

The work of this coach and teacher was a social one—two colleagues working together to improve instructional practices. This example illustrates that embedded in the conversation is reflective questioning and modeling where the coach and the teacher work to make sense of the events of the classroom from what was observed. This example also magnifies that for teachers to enact this type of collaboration there are skills that need to be developed—how to coach, how to engage in conversations that promote reflection, etc. Finally, this example highlights the importance of building relationships and trust as individual skill sets alone cannot support teacher growth. Peer coaching, reflection, and extended conversations about practices are the bedrock of collaborative professional learning processes.

Peer Coaching. Coaching and peer observations can take many forms and unfold in a variety of formats. Some systems have instructional coaches that focus efforts on literacy or mathematics, and these coaches are assigned to schools within the district. Some schools have a full-time coach in the building to support teachers and students in mathematics or literacy. In some schools, teachers engage in peer coaching where they work seamlessly with members of their teams observing each other's teaching, routinely modeling instructional practices. Often, through in-school mentoring programs, more experienced teachers conduct classroom observations to support the development of the school's newest members. The configurations of coaching are endless, and they need to be built to fit the context of the school and the needs of teachers.

Regardless of the configuration, peer coaching supports teachers as they implement new strategies and amplifies the benefits of other forms of professional development (Zepeda, 2019b). Peer coaching is not tied to teacher evaluation and is designed as a teacher-to-teacher model. The pioneering work of Joyce and Showers (1981, 2002) originally situated peer coaching as a follow-up to formal professional learning vis-a-vis modeling and classroom observations as ways to support teachers as they implemented strategies in their classrooms. Table 5.3 illustrates both peer coaching as a form of professional learning and as a stand-alone model of teacher support.

Reflection. Teachers grow their capacity for change when they reflect on their practices and what they are learning. Reflection between teachers enables them to ask questions, challenge each other's ideas, and think through ways in which they can improve their practices. Reflection can occur at the individual level; however, there is tremendous value and benefit when peers inquire and reflect collaboratively in pairs and in teams. Conversations provide unique opportunities that help teachers to reflect on their practice with colleagues.

Table 5.3 Peer Coaching Applications

Peer Coaching as a Professional Development Model	Peer Coaching as a Stand-Alone Process
Theory is presented	Pre-Observation Conference. The teacher and coach meet for a pre-observation conference to identify a focus for the observation.
Demonstration of the theory is presented	Classroom Observation. The coach observes the teacher.
Participants practice new skills	Post-Observation Conference. The teacher and coach meet to discuss data collected during the observation, identifying strengths and goals for growth, and planning next steps.
Feedback is given on the application of newly-learned skills	Subsequent cycles including observations are made.
Teachers are coached	Throughout the cycles, teachers engage in coaching for understanding and mastery.

Source: Adapted from Joyce and Showers (1981), Zepeda (2019b)

Extended Conversations. Conversations are not the chit-chat that occurs in hallways or the faculty lounge. Conversations are deep explorations of practice that enable teachers to reflect about their practices, envision new ones, and chart the course to change or modify instructional practices. There are many benefits associated with conversations as they help teachers to 1) build professional practices to improve instructional and classroom strategies, 2) reflect collectively on the work of teaching, 3) share professional knowledge and expertise, and 4) engage in fault-free discussions. Zepeda (2020) wrote that conversations matter because:

- *Conversations are about relationships*. Susan Scott (2004) reminds us that the conversation is the relationship and as such, teachers need opportunities to build relationships that can help reduce isolation (see Chapter 4). Conversations not only forge relationships, but they also provide support for teachers.

- *Conversations forge a sense of belonging*. Teachers believe they are a member of a team and that together, learning occurs through the exchange of ideas. As illustrated in Figure 1.1, a sense of belonging is necessary to build a positive school culture. When teachers sense that they belong, they are a part of a community that embraces multiple points-of-view, the varied experiences, and far-reaching support that can come from colleagues who are willing to engage in collaborative conversations, ask probing questions, and reflect about the impact of such efforts.

- *Conversations build a culture of learning.* A culture of learning supports teachers in becoming more satisfied, gaining more self-confidence, and deriving value from their own work and from working with others.

By working with others and engaging in deep and protracted conversations over time about teaching and learning, instructional practices, student work, and the impact of individual and collective efforts, teachers are willing to expose their vulnerabilities, weak spots, and the triumphant moments about what happens in classrooms. And this is why conversations need to be nestled in an environment that uplifts teachers and their efforts.

- *Conversations with colleagues focus in razor-like fashion on students and their learning.* In conversations embedded in classroom practices and the impact these practices have on student learning, teachers are in a position to learn through them. Students ultimately become the benefactors of teachers engaging in collaborative conversations about practices and their impact on learning. This is a bonus in that teachers and students learn as a result of these conversations.

- *Conversations embrace the principles of adult learning.* Adults want to study their practices and then through these explorations and conversations, they want to construct new knowledge based on what they have learned. A culture that promotes conversations fosters adult learning.

- *Conversations promote reflection.* Reflection supports teachers in making sense of the complexities of the classroom and the impact that their efforts have on students.

- *Conversations cultivate expertise.* Through conversations, teachers continuously build their skill sets and the confidence to share with colleagues.

Conversations, peer coaching, and reflection are supportive processes that extend earning opportunities for teachers to grow and to develop. When teachers engage in collaborative ways, the social capital of the schoolhouse increases its collective capacity as examined in Chapter 6.

Leading Culture

Understanding Culture and Professional Job-Embedded Learning

1. Conditions for sustained professional learning are specific and measurable (see Table 5.2) and must be at the forefront of organizational norms, values, and collective efficacy.

2. Coherence is achieved when strategies and processes are aligned to the content and purposes of professional learning.

3. Peer coaching, teacher reflection, and extended conversations are essential to teacher collaborative practices.

Leveraging the Power of Professional Job-Embedded Learning

1. How do your school's current professional learning practices align to the salient features of professional learning (see Table 5.2)?

2. In what ways can you measure the degree of coherence for teacher professional learning?

3. Identify opportunities for job-embedded professional learning that create the time and space for quality coaching, reflection, and collaboration.

Chapter Summary

The art and science of teaching is complex. Students are successful when teachers and leaders bring clarity and coherence to the work required to deliver effective instructional practices. While professional learning is often well intentioned, leaders must recognize that it does not always impact teacher practices or student outcomes. Effective professional learning must be collaborative and job-embedded with a focus on learning and reflection to enable professional growth.

Research has identified the professional learning elements that promote teacher collaboration and, subsequently, empower teacher voice, agency, trust, and growth. What are the elements? Leaders are responsible for identifying and reflecting how such elements are both evident and coherent in their schools. This learning must be job-embedded and reinforce professional practices aligned to teaching, learning, and student outcomes. Leaders are encouraged to reflect, in particular, about how the salient elements of professional learning can be embedded in peer coaching, reflection, and extended conversations.

Leading Practices

1. *Analyzing* professional learning in your school

    a. Refer to the salient features of professional learning in Table 5.2. In collaboration with teachers, assess which of these elements are consistently evident in your school.

2. *Developing Processes* to support a positive learning culture

    a. Initiate a process whereby teachers can establish organizational norms about how and when teacher collaboration will be job-embedded (compared to before/after school and on weekends).

3. *Implementing Strategies* that support a collaborative culture for learning

    a. Publicly commit to your staff the specifics of the time, space, and processes that will be initiated as a result of the review and subsequent implementation of research-based teacher collaborative and professional learning practices.

Suggested Readings

Knight, J. (2016). *Better conversations: Coaching ourselves and each other to be more credible, caring, and connected.* Corwin.

Zepeda, S. J. (2019). *Professional development: What works* (3rd ed.). Routledge.

Zepeda, S. J., Goff, L., & Steele, S. (2019). *C.R.A.F.T. conversations for teacher growth: How to build bridges and cultivate expertise*. Association of Supervision and Curriculum Development.

References

Calvert, L. (2016). The power of teacher agency. *Learning Forward, 37*(2), 51–56. https://learningforward.org/wp-content/uploads/2016/04/the-power-of-teacher-agency-april16.pdf

Darling-Hammond, L., Hyler, M. E., & Gardner, M. (2017). Effective teacher professional development. *Learning Policy Institute*. https://learningpolicyinstitute.org/sites/default/files/product-files/Effective_Teacher_Professional_Development_REPORT.pdf

Darling-Hammond, L., & Richardson, N. (2009). Teacher learning: What matters? *Educational Leadership, 66*(5), 46–53. www.ascd.org/publications/educational-

de Jong, L., Meirink, J., & Admiraal, W. (2019). School-based teacher collaboration: Different learning opportunities across various contexts. *Teaching and Teacher Education, 86*, 1–12. https://doi.org/10.1016/j.tate.2019.102925

Derrington, M. L., & Angelle, P. S. (2013). Teacher leadership and collective efficacy: Connections and links. *International Journal of Teacher Leadership, 4*(1), 1–13. www.csupomona.edu/~education/ijtl/issues.shtml.

Desimone, L. M. (2009). Improving impact studies of teachers' professional development: Toward better conceptualizations and measures. *Educational Researcher, 38*(3), 181–199. https://doi.org/10.3102%2F0013189X08331140

Desimone, L. M. (2011). A primer on professional development. *Phi Delta Kappan, 92*(6), 68–71. https://doi.org/10.1177%2F003172171109200616

Desimone, L. M., & Garet, M. S. (2015). Best practices in teachers' professional development in the United States. *Psychology, Society, and Education, 7*(3), 252–263. http://ojs.ual.es/ojs/index.php/psye

DuFour, R. (2006). Collaboration is the key to unlocking potential. *The Learning Principal, 2*(3), 1–8. https://learningforward.org/wp-content/uploads/2006/11/nov06-issue-1.pdf

Gates, S. (2018). Benefits of collaboration. *National Education Association*. www.nea.org/professional-excellence/student-engagement/tools-tips/benefits-collaboration

Goddard, Y. L., Goddard, R. D., & Tschannen-Moran, M. (2007). A theoretical and empirical investigation of teacher collaboration for school improvement and student achievement in public elementary schools. *Teachers College Record, 109*(4), 877–896. www.tcrecord.org/Content.asp?ContentId=12871

Goddard, Y. L., Miller, R., Larsen, R., Goddard, R., Madsen, J., & Schroeder, P. (2010). Connecting principal leadership, teacher collaboration, and student achievement. A paper presented at *the Annual Meeting of the American Educational Research Association*, Denver, CO. https://files.eric.ed.gov/fulltext/ED528704.pdf

Hargreaves, A. (2019). Teacher collaboration: 30 years of research on its nature, forms, limitations and effects. *Teachers and Teaching, 25*(5), 603–621. https://doi.org/10.1080/13540602.2019.1639499

Hargreaves, A., & O'Connor, M. T. (2017). Cultures of professional collaboration: The origins and opponents. *Journal of Professional Capital and Community, 2*(2), 74–85. https://doi.org/10.1108/JPCC-02-2017-0004

Jensen, B., Sonnemann, J., Roberts-Hull, K., & Hunter, A. (2016). *Beyond PD: Teacher professional learning in high-performing systems*. National Center on Education and the Economy.

Johnston, W. R., & Tsai, T. (2018). *The prevalence of collaboration among American teachers: National findings from the American Teacher Panel*. RAND. https://doi.org/10.7249/RR2217

Joyce, B., & Showers, B. (1981). Transfer of training: The contribution of "coaching". *Journal of Education, 163*(2), 163–172. www.jstor.org/stable/42772926

Joyce, B., & Showers, B. (2002). *Student achievement through staff development*. Association for Supervision and Curriculum Development.

Mora-Ruano, J. G., Heine, J. H., & Gebhardt, M. (2019). Does teacher collaboration improve student achievement? Analysis of the German PISA

2012 sample. *Frontiers in Education, 4*, 1–12. https://doi.org/10.3389/feduc.2019.00085

Morel, N. J. (2014). Setting the stage for collaboration: An essential skill for professional growth. *Delta Kappa Gamma Bulletin, 81*(1), 36–39. www.dkg.org/DKGMember/Publications/Journal/DKGMember/Publications/Bulletin-Journal.aspx?

O'Neil, M. (2018). *Collaborative leadership and 7 other traits strong leaders have.* Promises at Work. www.samewave.com/posts/collaborative-leadership-and-7-other-traits-strong-leaders-have

Psunder, M. (2009). Collaborative culture as a challenge of contemporary schools. *Problems of Education in the 21st Century, 14*, 84. www.scientiasocialis.lt/pec/node/files/pdf/Psunder_Vol.14.pdf

Pugach, M. C., Blanton, L. P., Correa, V. I., McLeskey, J., & Langley, L. K. (2009). *The role of collaboration in supporting the induction and retention of new special education teachers.* National Center to Inform Policy and Practice in Special Education Professional Development. http://ncipp.education.ufl.edu/files_6/NCIPP%20Collab_010310.pdf

Ronfeldt, M., Farmer, S. O., McQueen, K., & Grissom, J. A. (2015). Teacher collaboration in instructional teams and student achievement. *American Educational Research Journal, 52*(3), 475–514. https://doi.org/10.3102/0002831215585562

Scott, S. (2004). *Fierce conversations: Achieving success at work & in life, one conversation at a time.* Berkley Publishing Group.

Stanhope, N. (2020). Conditions for collaboration—Part 1: When it's really hard. *Medium.* https://medium.com/digitalfund/conditions-for-collaboration-part-1-when-its-really-hard-ad8ef7e20187

Sutton, P. S., & Shouse, A. W. (2016). Building a culture of collaboration in schools. *Phi Delta Kappan, 97*(7), 69–73. https://doi.org/10.1177/0031721716641653

ThoughtFarmer. (2021, February). *What collaboration really means.* www.thoughtfarmer.com/blog/what-collaboration-really-means/

Zepeda, S. J. (2015). *Job-embedded professional development: Support, collaboration, and learning in schools.* Routledge.

Zepeda, S. J. (2019a). Job-embedded professional learning: Federal legislation and national reports as levers. In M. L. Derrington & J. Brandon

(Eds.), *Differentiated teacher evaluation and professional learning: Policies and practices for promoting teacher career growth*. Palgrave Publishing.

Zepeda, S. J. (2019b). *Professional development: What works* (3rd ed.). Routledge.

Zepeda, S. J. (2020, September). Crafting conversations for teacher growth [Blog]. *The Expat Leader*. www.magzter.com

The Social Dynamics That Build School Culture

Examining School Culture

A school district has experienced a yearly decline in annual enrollment to its four elementary schools. After much deliberation, the decision was made to close one of the schools and to consolidate from three elementary schools to one elementary school. The district transferred faculty members from each of the three schools to a new large elementary school. They hired a new principal to lead a new faculty in developing a model of strong teacher collaboration. Collaboration was important because each of the closed schools had a faculty that worked independently. The district anticipated that the leader would need to first focus on developing relationships and a model of collaboration and trust.

The superintendent was well aware of the challenges the principal would face in bringing an experienced faculty together and developing a collaborative model which was in alignment to the district's direction. The reassigned teachers in the schools that closed reflected an average slightly over 10 years' experience with 50% of the teachers having taught in only the schools that closed.

The new principal's strength was in developing school culture founded on building relationships. He understood the need to develop a plan about how the faculty would "enter" the new consolidated school. The underpinning of the plan was to build the confidence of teachers by empowering them to take ownership and hold responsibility for *all* students. Teacher leadership was essential to build human and social capital.

Introduction

Improving schools and the achievement of students has always been at the center of educational conversations—all with great intentions of finding answers. Unfortunately, seeking the answers traditionally resided in examining metrics to measure success such as test scores and their distillation to measure a teacher's effectiveness to numerical scores coupled with threats to release teachers from their jobs and to strip them of their teaching credentials. The center of school improvement was shouldered on the effectiveness of individual teachers as well as school leaders. All of which created nominal evidence that these school improvement efforts and attempts to improve teacher effectiveness changed the outcomes for students.

The approach to improve schools has shifted away from the accountability measures associated with the No Child Left Behind (2002) movement. With schools experiencing little improvement, school leaders are renewing conversations to build capacity by developing school culture through teacher ownership and the professional interactions between teachers and leaders.

This chapter examines the importance of teacher ownership and collective responsibility to develop a culture that builds and sustains school capacity. The focus on human and social capital is warranted to build capacity.

School Capacity

While school capacity is often viewed as broad and ubiquitous, building school capacity in the context of culture describes the individual and collective work in creating an environment centered on skills, practices, abilities, and the expertise needed to meet expectations for students (Education Reform, 2013). School capacity is created, in part, by embracing collective teacher and leader ownership and by recognizing the collective responsibilities needed to bring clarity to these efforts.

Collective Ownership

The history of education reforms and innovations have been plagued by the introduction of school improvement practices that lack sustainability and are short lived within the school's culture. Too often, reform efforts to improve school achievement fail because school practices have been either top down driven or mandated through local, state, and national policies. In many instances, teachers were the last to know about the changes that would impact their effectiveness in the classroom.

The foundation of successful schools is created when those within the school have either a direct or indirect role in decisions that impact effectiveness. When teachers are engaged in processes to ensure good decisions, they become supportive and feel a sense of pride and ownership. When decisions are made that are top down or function through mandates, the end result creates fractures within the faculty and strong tensions between teachers and between teachers and leaders.

Furthermore, changes in schools are often less effective due to the focus on the change itself rather than on how teachers influence efforts to innovate practices. According to Saunders et al. (2017), "When improvement initiatives give teachers little control or opportunity to provide input and are perceived as ephemeral, teachers' ability to carry out the initiative effectively may be weakened" (p. 1). The importance of teacher engagement and agency are central to the success of long-term reform efforts. It is through engagement that collective ownership evolves.

Understanding the conditions required for teachers to engage in improvement efforts and feel ownership requires leaders to pay close attention to teachers and the alignment of their beliefs and their ability to have impact. Saunders et al. (2017) position that "teacher ownership is a powerful construct with the potential to create meaningful school and system change" (p. 37). Moreover, Saunders et al. (2017) report that teacher ownership:

- Takes root in environments where teachers can work together, learn from each other, spread knowledge and ideas, and lead improvement efforts.

- Takes time to develop.

- Requires creating balance between classroom responsibilities and efforts to contribute to the collective.

- Cultivates greater investment in students' learning, school outcomes, and the community.

- Acknowledges teachers' expertise, knowledge, and skills.

(p. 37)

In schools with a positive culture, sustained innovation and change evolve because leaders empower teachers to engage in decision making.

Leaders are critical in developing school practices that create a culture of teacher ownership. To support the development of this type of culture, leaders provide:

1. *Clarity and agreement in the school's direction.* Teacher beliefs need to be aligned to the core beliefs of the school, its values, and aspirations for both students and the adults. Questions and differences will arise on "how" the work gets done but with agreement in directions, the question about the "why" the work remains constant and consistent. (See Chapter 5)

2. *Support for teacher collaboration.* Foundational to developing a collaborative culture is providing the time needed for teachers to engage in formal and informal conversations. Collaborative models are created through a shared set of beliefs that lay the foundation for building community, establishing metrics for accountability, and engaging in professional conversations that lead to best practices. (See Chapter 4)

3. *Promote leadership roles for teachers outside of the classroom.* Teachers as leaders bring much experience not only to the classroom but also in the overall success of the school. Leaders develop teacher

leaders by promoting and creating opportunities that tap into their interests, knowledge, and experiences. (See Chapter 4 and later in this chapter)

4. *Opportunities for peer observation and discussion.* Peer observations create opportunities for teachers to learn with each other and to gain powerful insights about their own practice. Peer observations support honest discussions about instructional practices, provide multiple views in solving problems, encourage reflection, and develop teacher confidence. (See Chapter 5)

5. *Professional learning opportunities developed and led by teachers.* Teachers have a deep reservoir of expertise that has tremendous value when they are engaged in professional learning with their colleagues. Peer learning opportunities are relevant to a teacher's professional needs, require professional trust and create intrinsic value in their work with peers and their students. (See Chapters 4 and 5)

The attention to teacher influence and ownership of their own individual and school-wide processes plays a pivotal role as schools seek to build a culture of capacity through collective ownership that leads to collective responsibility.

Collective Responsibility

Albeit complex, the basic premise of collective responsibility in schools is when teachers and leaders *together* assume mutual ownership for their decisions and the resulting outcomes. Furthermore, Lee and Smith (1996) determined that "achievement gains are significantly higher in schools where teachers take collective responsibility for students' academic success or failure rather than blaming students for their own failure" (p. 103). Similarly, best practices to improve achievement in turnaround schools reflect "Administrators and teachers are jointly committed to and have assumed shared ownership and collective responsibility for improving student achievement" (Massachusetts Department of Elementary and Secondary Education, 2016, p. 4).

Creating a culture of collective responsibility begins by examining leader and teacher beliefs about students. First, leaders and teachers need to accept that it is their responsibility together to challenge and ensure the success for every student. The second is the belief that all students can learn at high levels and that they are prepared to be lifelong learners (Solution Tree, 2018). Furthermore, collective responsibility is fostered when teachers care about each other's success and are willing to share their expertise (Hirsh, 2010).

Developing a school culture of collective responsibility may have the most significant impact on school improvement. Too often, the impact of reform efforts and new institutional practices become short-lived or their impact never realized due to internal and external divisions and lack of ownership. The "power of one voice" where leaders and teachers take joint responsibility for change within their schools has a significant impact on their collective work.

Collective responsibility of teachers and leaders creates the undercarriage for teacher growth and development while underscoring the value of taking ownership of teaching and learning. In positive cultures, school leaders and teachers commit to values, beliefs, and the actions to leverage best practices that create a positive learning culture (see Chapters 3 and 5). Through common understanding of school-wide commitments, leaders and teachers become united in employing the best practices for all students to succeed. Table 6.1 examines the relationships between collective responsibility and the commitments that need to be made to build and sustain a positive school culture.

Table 6.1 Collective Responsibility and the Commitments to a Positive Culture

Collective Responsibilities All teachers share a commitment . . .	Commitments to a Positive Culture In a positive school culture . . .
To the achievement of all students.	All students achieve at high levels when they are in a culture where all teachers believe in their abilities and uniqueness.
To support individual teachers in their attempt to ensure the success of students.	Individual teachers can better help students who are not achieving in a culture where they can get needed support from colleagues.
To share what is working in their classrooms with their colleagues.	All students benefit in a culture where all teachers use best practices that are tested and shared.

Collective Responsibilities *All teachers share a commitment . . .*	Commitments to a Positive Culture *In a positive school culture . . .*
To support less experienced teachers in realizing that other teachers are invested in their success and the success of all students.	All students benefit in a culture where all teachers, regardless of experience, employ effective instructional practices.
To learn and work together systematically on a regular basis to collectively ensure higher quality instruction in all classrooms and better results for all students.	All students benefit when the culture of the school is founded on continuous teacher collaboration resulting in the use of effective and quality instructional practices.
To team-based professional learning embedded in their work schedule.	All teachers grow and develop in ways to support all students when principals realize the power of a professional learning culture where teacher teams engage in ongoing professional learning.

Source: Adapted from Hirsh (2010)

Making commitments and being responsible to them brings schools together in ways that focus and harness the talents and expertise within the system. A laser focus on creating collective action and responsibility evolves when efforts are coherent.

Coherence

The work of schools within a system is complicated, especially since many of the day-to-day decisions that directly impact leaders, teachers, students, and parents are made at the system level. Critically important for leaders and teachers is understanding how system and school coherence, or lack of, is impacted by decisions, outcomes, and the culture of the school. Coherence between central office and schools and coherence between school leaders and teachers is created through strategic processes by superintendents and school leaders. However, the voice and agency of teachers at the ground level has one of the greatest impacts on aligning and sustaining initiatives that support the direction of the system.

The responsibility for ensuring system coherence lies squarely on the shoulders of the superintendent. With system coherence, district actions become predictable and bring sustainability to initiatives and programs. As districts navigate an ever-changing environment, system coherence also supports school leaders in being more efficient, less fragmented, and better prepared to effectively leverage resources and the use of time (Zepeda et al., 2021). Furthermore, "changes in the system are sustained and become part of the culture when leaders understand how the power of unity can bring coherence across many moving parts" (Lanoue & Zepeda, 2018, p. 162).

Creating district and school cultures that reflect system coherence requires not only alignment, but also the use of processes that engage and create meaning. While everyone in the district may be able to articulate the system direction, the translation into action often varies across schools and individuals. Instead of assuming everyone is on the same page, deliberate attempts must be made to build a culture developed from a deep and shared understanding of purpose (Srinivasan & Archer, 2018).

According to Hatch (2015), "common understanding and coherence grows out of the connections and relationships among people that facilitate the flow of information, resources and knowledge" that makes it possible for individuals and groups to coordinate their activities and develop a common sense of what they are supposed to do and why they are doing it (p. 105). The ability for schools to be cohesive and effective in their work requires engagement through teacher voice and change through teacher agency in creating a culture of collective action and ownership.

Teaching and learning is a human endeavor that develops positive human dynamics within schools, where everyone is moving in the same direction, and is one of the most critical requirements for successful school leaders. Leading with coherence requires intentionality in creating the conditions required for developing and maintaining human capital.

Leading Culture

Understanding Culture

1. Teacher ownership for school culture and improvement occurs through specific, sustained practices that encourage agency and engagement.

2. Collective responsibility is developed when teachers and leaders lead together resulting in gains in student achievement.

3. Coherence is achieved when all individuals and groups have a common purpose and goals for achievement.

Leveraging the Power of Culture

1. Identify the practices in your school that contribute to a culture of collective teacher ownership.

2. What evidence do you have in your school to show teachers and leaders take collective responsibility for practices leading to student's academic success or failure (rather than blaming students for their own failure)?

3. To what degree does coherence exist between district and school leadership and teachers relative to school improvement and teacher agency?

Human Capital

It's one thing to develop human capital but another thing to harness it through social capital. Human capital is considered generally the assets of the individual that bring value to the setting (Amadeo & Boyle, 2021) whereas social capital, according to the review provided by Bridwell-Mitchell and Cooc (2016), is defined as the "potential and actual set of cognitive, social, and material resources made available through direct and indirect relationships with others" (p. 7). Both human and social capital are important to building a positive school culture. Although collaboration and professional learning (see Chapter 6) and relationships (see Chapter 4) are examined in previous chapters, the focus here is on the relationship of a positive school culture to building and developing human and social capital. The impact of human capital on student achievement is bolstered exponentially through social capital.

Historically, public sentiment and the push for teacher accountability has called for a stronger, more competent teacher in every classroom. The trail following reform efforts set out to "fix" broken schools and that by "upgrading the human capital in low-performing schools will improve the performance of those schools" (King Rice & Malen, 2003, p. 635). Emanating from this mindset were tactics and strategies including the turnaround movement where schools that did not meet targets were taken over and teachers and leaders—the building-level human capital—were removed. Fast forward to 2009 and the U.S. Department of Education *Race to the Top* (RTT) agenda also called for school reconstitution as a turnaround strategy for underperforming schools (Goldstein, 2014; Hansen, 2013). The adage, in desperate times, people engage in desperate activities, held true here—in knee-jerk fashion, human capital would be lost.

Srivastava and Das (2015) offer an encompassing definition of human capital: "Human capital is a collection of resources, it comprises all [of] the knowledge, talents, skills, abilities, experience, intelligence, judgment, and wisdom possessed individually and collectively by individuals" (para 1). Put another way, Beaver and Weinbaum (2012) delineate that "human capital is the amount that a school benefits from having each individual working there, each person with his or her own strengths, weaknesses, and preferences" (p. 3).

With these definitions, human capital are the assets that teachers bring to the school or are developed by programs and efforts of the school and its system. Teachers come to the schoolhouse with human capital. For example, regardless of experience, teachers have earned college degrees, and they have engaged in professional learning. Developing human capital is achieved by investing in professional learning that could include sending teachers to advanced training in working with students and families in poverty or focused professional development on new math standards. Moreover, human capital is developed even further when learning is embedded in the workday (see Chapter 5 discussion about professional job-embedded learning).

Building capacity comes with an individual and collective sense of ownership and responsibility for students, teachers, leaders and all others who comprise the school. In the past, human capital was a term that signaled the economic and investment structures of the labor force (Coleman, 1988; Goldin, 2001); a knowledge economy (Mokyr, 2004); production functions of the use of resources, cost effectiveness, and student outcomes (Crocker, 2006; Hanushek, 1989); human resource management as a function of the central office (Crocker, 2006; Zepeda et al., 2021); and for this discussion, school leaders at the site (Myung et al., 2013).

Human capital is further developed at the school level when leaders:

- find time and resources for teachers to collaborate;
- secure convenient but high-quality professional development opportunities to meet professional goals;
- promote a "learning anytime, anywhere" going beyond "just-in-time" learning often offered episodically when a deficit is discovered;
- leverage existing programs at the site including mentoring and induction; teacher evaluation systems; and,
- promote the development of teacher leadership.

The collective learning of teachers within the school supports building both the individual and the human capital of the collective. The possibilities for developing human capital are endless. Induction, mentoring, and teacher leadership are examined as ways to build capital.

Induction

From a system level, districts invest in human capital through their efforts to recruit, induct, and retain teachers—the human capital—assigned to teach. For perspective, personnel expenditures are the highest line-item in any school district, making up approximately 80% or more of a budget (Myung et al., 2013). Moreover, the teaching workforce is now less experienced with a modality of one to three years' experience in 2016 which is a substantive change from 15 years of experience in 1988 (Ingersoll, 2018). In Chapter 2, teacher retention and attritions were examined briefly illustrating that it is difficult to build a positive school culture when there is a revolving door of teachers being hired only to spend a short time at the school site. Issues related to attrition and teacher shortages have caused staffing problems in PreK-12 public schools necessitating an increased need for improving teacher induction, especially since there is a strong link between quality induction programs and higher teacher retention rates (Gamborg et al., 2018; Ronfeldt & McQueen, 2017).

The "Why" behind induction is apparent. Almost every early-career teacher struggles learning a range of instructional practices; the complexities of working with students, the dynamics of working with teachers, policies, procedures, new curriculum standards, grading, and a host of other "firsts" in their careers. In addition, too many new teachers (44%) leave the profession within their first five years in the classroom (Ingersoll, 2018). For these reasons and more, induction is an essential part of building teacher capacity. The first few years of teaching lay the foundation for future success and longevity in the profession. Feiman-Nemser et al. (1999) predicted that for early career teachers, the induction years predict "what kind of teacher they become" (p. 1).

Induction supports play an instrumental role in socializing early career teachers as they acclimate, becoming members of the school and their role in it (Alhija & Fresko, 2016). The support provided through induction efforts for early-career teachers helps them to bridge what was learned in their preparation programs with assuming full responsibilities as a class-room teacher. It is through the induction period that early career teachers are able to make sense of the school culture, experience the ethos of care and concern for their well-being, and feel a sense of belonging to the com-munity so through the support of peers they can "confront the dichotomy of theory and practice in all its intensity" (Warford, 2011, p. 255).

Leaders support induction when they purposefully connect resources, time, and energy toward bridging the gaps of formal preparation. Support is not a series of happenstance events. Leaders create opportunities for new teachers to observe other teachers in their classrooms and provide time for them to engage in conversations about what was observed. Professional learning opportunities would be differentiated to meet the needs of the newest members of the school community. A strong mentoring component embedded through interactions with experienced colleagues provides new teachers to the school with timely support.

Mentoring

Mentoring is about building human capital for the schools' newest members—early career teachers. Mentoring is more often associated with the induction of early career teachers; however, mentoring is a support that can be implemented formally and informally for all teachers, regardless of their experience levels. More experienced teachers new to a school, experienced teachers who are teaching new content, and experienced teachers who are having difficulties with a specific grouping of students can also benefit from the coaching and support of a mentor teacher.

Mentorship is a professional and trusting relationship where experienced teachers (mentors) collaborate, set goals, and solve problems with new teachers (mentees) in the workplace (Carr et al., 2017; DeCesare et al., 2016). Mentors engage teachers in on-going and supportive social interactions. Mentors provide critical guidance and develop future on-the-job learning opportunities that cover broad topics in classroom management, and planning for instruction (Hong & Matsko, 2019). Mentors also model professionalism, provide social emotional support, and help early-career teachers navigate the political landscape of the school and its community.

More seasoned teachers ease the entry of recent graduates into teaching when they serve as mentors. Mentors help to cultivate human capital as they guide and support the work with new teachers. Induction and mentoring efforts support, in reciprocal ways, human capital development for both the more experienced teacher who serves as a mentor and the early career teacher.

Mentoring has been shown to be an effective practice for helping early career teachers to:

- improve their pedagogical skills (Fenwick, 2011; Sutcher et al., 2019);
- make sense of the dynamics of students they are assigned to teach (Hudson, 2012);
- become socialized helping early career teachers become "familiar with school norms and procedures, assisting them with adapting to the school culture, aiding them in instructional planning and classroom management, and providing constructive feedback on their teaching through formative evaluations" (Alhija & Fresko, 2016, p. 18);
- combat isolation (Hong & Matsko, 2019) and increases a sense of belonging (Zepeda, 2018); and,
- increase commitment to the profession (Hong & Matsko, 2019).

Mentoring helps early career teachers find their voice, reflect on practice, and develop the agency to make decisions (see Chapter 1). Through the guidance of a mentor, early career teachers develop decision-making skills. Mentors not only provide critical information but they also model professional dispositions as they work with early career teachers.

In developing successful mentoring programs, leaders should pay particular attention to

- mentor selection, mentor assignment, mentor training, and the ongoing professional development that mentors need to enact this work with early career teachers;
- time, granting release time for mentors and early career teachers to meet; and,
- the resources that can be leveraged from the central office to support efforts.

Effective leaders acknowledge that they do not always have the time necessary or expertise to mentor and induct teachers without the support of experienced teachers.

Teacher Leadership

Teachers build and accumulate expertise and knowledge over time in the profession by how they lead every day in the classroom. In strong school cultures, principals cultivate teacher leadership beyond the walls of individual classrooms (see also, Chapter 4). The definition of teacher leadership and the roles that they assume are elusive and go back to the context of the schools, the ways in which principals support the development of leadership, the history of teacher leadership in the building, and so forth (Wenner & Campbell, 2017).

Katzenmeyer and Moller (2009) suggest that teacher leaders "influence others toward improved educational practice; and accept responsibility for achieving the outcomes of their leadership" (p. 6). Teacher leadership will only thrive in a healthy school culture marked by relational trust, collective responsibility, a commitment to continuous development, and where teachers are recognized and celebrated for the expertise they share with others (Killion et al., 2016).

Teacher leaders influence, guide, and are situated at the center of practice—practices to improve teaching and learning and practices to improve professional relationships with teachers and between teachers and leaders. It is not so much about the formal or informal roles that are cast for teacher leaders. Rather, it is more important that teacher leadership is embedded as a part of a culture of support (York-Barr & Duke, 2004) where leadership is more distributed (Neumerski, 2013; Spillane, 2012); and where structures are in place to support teacher leaders including release time and leadership skill development (Nguyen & Hunter, 2018). Teacher leadership that is embedded as part of the work for all teachers will yield more capacity for the collective of the school.

Principals create opportunities for teachers to be leaders by:

1. tapping into their expertise by enlisting their decision-making to solve school-wide problems.

2. supporting their professional learning around being a teacher leader. This type of development could include, for example, pairing a more established teacher leader to mentor a less-experienced one.

3. providing timely feedback to teacher leaders about their leadership practices. Feedback embedded in conversations will support the growth and development of leadership skills.

4. providing opportunities for teacher leaders to develop, design, and lead professional learning at the site (by grade-level, whole-school), across the district, and beyond at local and national associations.

5. creating structures and time for teacher leaders to connect with teachers to engage in mentoring, peer observations with those new to teaching or to the school.

6. supporting teacher innovation and risk taking.

Principals support the development of teacher leaders as a major way to build individual and collective human capital. The types of relationships that teacher leaders broker can add exponentially to the efforts of principals to build and sustain social capital.

Leading Culture

Understanding Culture

1. Teacher induction can serve as a bridge between teacher preparation programs and school classrooms, whereby teachers can make sense of school culture, experience a concern for the well-being of colleagues, and develop a sense of community.

2. Mentoring occurs when new teachers collaborate with an experienced teacher to establish goals, plan lessons, and solve problems together.

3. Teacher leaders influence their colleagues to improve educational practice and accept collective responsibility for improved outcomes.

Leveraging the Power of Culture

1. How do your teacher induction practices invite a teacher into the culture of the school (rather than just clarify operational tasks)?

2. Identify ways in which teacher mentoring is supported by school leaders relative to time, resources, and the identification of quality mentors.

3. How is teacher leadership strategically nurtured at your school to build individual and collective capacity?

 # Social Capital

In educational improvement efforts, a major focus has been on building the human capital of individual teachers gained through formal education, experiences, and professional learning. However, understanding the value of social capital, what is gained through relationships and the sharing of ideas and information between teachers and leaders, is critical in building school capacity. Social capital is developed by increasing knowledge through the interactions with peers. Coherence of efforts to build social capital "serves an interpersonal purpose—the way teachers make sense of their work, the work of others, and the relationship to the system" (Zepeda et al., 2021, p. 25). Hargreaves and Fullan (2012) explain that social capital:

> refers to how the quantity and quality of interactions and social relationships among people affects their access to knowledge and information; their senses of expectation, obligation and trust; and how far they are likely to adhere to the same norms or codes of behavior.

> (p. 90)

Social capital plays a pivotal role in increasing knowledge because it "gives you access to other people's *human capital*. It expands your networks of influence and opportunity. And it develops resilience when you know there are people to go to who can give you advice and be your advocates" (Hargreaves & Fullan, 2012, p. 90, emphasis in the original).

Social capital has been defined as the intangible resources and the social connections that can be accessed to create action (Lin, 2001); form professional learning communities (Moolenaar & Sleegers, 2014); serve as a predictor of organizational performance and instructional quality (Leana & Pil, 2006); and increase teacher quality (Hargreaves & Fullan, 2012). Social capital builds assets such as collaboration where teachers can work with one another; where they can innovate; and where they experience a sense of belonging as illustrated in Figure 1.1—and the unifying elements to a positive school culture (see Chapter 1).

Hargreaves and Fullan (2012) explain that building social capital supports school improvement in that "Every time you increase the purposeful learning of teachers working together, you get both short-term results and longer term benefits as teachers learn the value of their peers and come to appreciate the worth of constructive disagreement" (p. 91). Leaders build social capital when they:

- value teacher expertise (Penuel et al., 2009);
- actively shape the school environment by cueing into its culture (Drago-Severson & Blum-DeStefano, 2014; Louis et al., 2013); and,
- focus leadership efforts on instruction (Drago-Severson & Blum-DeStefano, 2014; Zepeda et al., 2017).

For school leaders, paying attention to social capital is an important aspect of school improvement.

Relationship to Human Capital

Social capital and human capital are interdependent and Beaver and Weinbaum (2012) illustrate this connection: "social capital is closely linked to human capital—without social capital, the skills and expertise of staff are not shared and therefore remain trapped at the individual level and cannot be leveraged for ongoing organizational improvement" (p. 3).

Social capital supports the diffusion of human capital to the larger collective of the school.

In schools that experience a high degree of teacher turnover, a gap occurs in its social capital. When teachers leave, knowledge and relationships in the schoolhouse end and the dynamics of the school and its culture are impacted. The human capital that teachers brought to the school as well as the capital gained through professional learning leaves with them. When teachers and leaders leave, the system must focus on filling the gaps caused by the loss of personnel. These gaps are in teacher and leader knowledge and expertise as well as the negative impact that the turnover has on students.

Leading through a culture lens for school stability and improvement requires an understanding of how social and human capital impact the system and the work of teachers. Building and maintaining social and human capital through social networks requires leaders to be intentional in shaping relationships (Moolenaar & Sleegers, 2015).

Social Networks

Strong school cultures are built, in large part, by systems in place to support teacher voice and agency. Collective responsibility, ownership for student success, and teacher development falls in line with what is known about building human capital and its relationship to social capital. For leaders to develop a positive culture, they need to further leverage social capital by creating opportunities for teachers to develop solutions by exercising agency in collaboration with others (see Chapter 1). Leveraging capital coupled with social networks can lead to more positive outcomes with the implementation of reform strategies often associated with change and school improvement efforts (Penuel et al., 2010).

Social networks are more than just contacts or a collection of people that form into a group. Social networks connect people, and they do so through collaboration (Moolenaar et al., 2012). In social networks, knowledge is shared, people are connected to one another, practices are examined and solutions to complex issues are unpacked. Examining networks in schools requires focus on both knowledge exchange and the "the pattern of relationships between educators in a bounded group that reflects their purposive interaction" with one another (Moolenaar &

Sleegers, 2015, p. 11). Without collaboration and trust nestled in an environment where relationships and belonging are valued, social networks cannot support teacher learning and growth.

What happens in and through social networks influences who teachers go to for support, how they engage in problem-solving, and what resources are available. Human resources are embedded in social capital that make-up social networks. In fact, social capital is a vital resource that can be tapped to build capacity, forge a sense of belonging, empower teachers to exert agency, and foster a strong sense of efficacy (see Chapter 1). It is this capital that populates social networks that evolve in schools.

Social networks are fostered through strong personal and professional relationships and collaboration. Social networks add value, and they build school capacity. Social networks build expertise through the collective of the network that can support teachers in solving the complex problems they encounter. Leaders that focus on building culture leverage efforts through the attention to teachers' needs by focusing on their continuous intellectual development that is dependent on social interactions (Moolenaar & Sleegers, 2015). Moreover, leaders who are attuned to their faculty are better positioned to share and align the school's vision and provide timely and supportive resources. Through this type of engagement, leaders are able to encourage solidarity among network members, develop a shared language, establish common values, and create an agreed upon vision for the school (Claridge, 2019).

The glue of social networks is the ties that bind teachers to one another and to their work. It is through these ties that teachers feel connected to one another and where information and more is shared. Hangül and Şentürk (2019) elaborate that *"ties* act as pipelines by which advice, friendship, information, behaviors, beliefs, [and] materials . . . could be transferred to influence behaviors" of members (p. 17, emphasis added). The ties between individuals are important and cannot be ignored by school leaders because culture is created and vetted through human interactions embedded in the workings of social networks.

There are two types of social networks—formal and informal ones. In formal social networks, attention is paid to defined responsibilities. A formal social network could include, for example, a team or grade level at the school. At the system level, a formal social network could consist of all grade-level or subject-matter teachers in the district. Formal networks typically have more structured functions, meet regularly, and oversight is governed by appointment. However, formal social networks can be collaboratively led.

Informal social networks evolve organically within schools and their systems. Informal social networks could be based on interest or need, and they can branch out from formal social networks. For example, in a formal social network of ninth-grade English teachers, several teachers are in their first year in the system. These teachers branch out developing their own social network of support. This network of teachers has different needs that are specific to not only teaching English but also needs associated with facing the first year of teaching. This network would more than likely share curricular materials but more than likely give support, encouragement, and work on creating a sense of belonging among its members.

Over time, commitments shape the inner workings of social network group members. Values and norms support social network members as they structure their work (see Chapters 3 and 4). Creating and maintaining social networks that support individual and collective capacity requires leaders to understand the uniqueness of their system—the history, the internal and external influences, and changing internal dynamics within the faculty and staff. When dynamics change dramatically, social ties change as well. When social ties change, so too do social networks. This point is illustrated when a school experiences a high turn-over rate of its teachers. When teachers leave so too does their expertise and the ties that these teachers had with members of the social networks found in the school.

Social networks are not static—they change over time as the needs of the school or the members change. Teachers gain expertise in an area so the focus of the social network pivots to look at other areas or the interests of the members. Social networks are important in that they can provide a safe space where teachers can help each other through the development of solutions to problems and engage in discussions that support innovation and refinement of ideas and practices.

Strategically, leaders need to understand how to influence these networks in ways to build important social capital. Social networks connect the skills and knowledge of individuals with the skills and expertise of their peers. Social capital is built when:

1. Members have access to effective instructional practices and resources to improve instructional delivery.

2. Teachers within the school interface with outside networks.

3. Members hold high levels of trust when working with each other and hold positive intentions.

(Gordon et al., 2016)

Social networks create powerful opportunities to establish critical social capital to improve teaching and learning.

Leading Culture

Understanding Culture

1. Social capital is developed by increasing knowledge through interactions with peers.

2. When schools experience a high degree of teacher turnover, gaps occur in its social capital that negatively impact teacher relationships, professional learning, and school improvement efforts.

3. Social networks in a school—the formal and the informal, the professional and the personal—connect teachers to one another and their work.

Leveraging the Power of Culture

1. Reflect on the intangible resources and social connections that contribute to the social capital that exist in your building.

2. Given the reality of teacher attrition, how does your school proactively manage the potential loss of teacher leadership, knowledge, and relationships?

3. In what ways do you encourage formal and informal social networks in your building to support the network of social capital?

Chapter Summary

School capacity, human capital, and social capital each contribute to the foundation of school improvement. Leaders can develop teacher ownership and collective accountability through a variety of strategies, including but not limited to clarity and agreement in the school's direction, support for teacher collaboration, teacher leadership opportunities outside the classroom, and peer observation and discussion. Coherence is achieved when all levels of the organization—district, school, and classroom—have a shared understanding of vision and purpose. Put simply, people know what they need to do and why they need to do it.

Human capital recognizes the value that each person brings to the organization and how the school benefits from having the person work there. Strategies to improve individual and collective human capital include teacher induction programs, mentoring relationships, and teacher leadership opportunities. For each, it is critically important that leaders demonstrate a value for teacher expertise, create a sense of individual and shared purpose, and nurture teacher collaboration. Social capital, which is inextricably linked to human capital, can also be leveraged to expand a teacher's network of influence and opportunity. Networks, both formal and informal, insulate schools from teacher turnover and subsequent gaps in professional expertise and sense of belonging.

Leading Practices

1. *Analyzing* school improvement and cultural coherence

    a. Identify the most critical school improvement priority/process in your school/system and seek input regarding the degree of coherence within the school's culture (individually and collectively).

2. *Developing Processes* needed to create a culture of teacher development and support

    a. Initiate a process (or improve an existing process) that supports a culture of teacher induction, mentoring, and teacher leadership.

3. *Implementing Strategies* to build human and social capital

    a. Engage in conversations with your staff to determine how they perceive opportunities to foster human and social capacity within your system/school.

Suggested Readings

Drago-Severson, E., & Blum-DeStefano, J. (2018). *Leading change together: Developing educator capacity within schools and systems*. Association of Supervision and Curriculum Development.

Hargreaves, A., & Fullan, M. (2012). *Professional capital: Transforming teaching in every school*. Teachers College Press.

Perret, K., & McKee, K. (2021). *Compassionate coaching: How to help educators navigate barriers to professional growth*. Association of Supervision and Curriculum Development.

References

Alhija, F. M., & Fresko, B. (2016). A retrospective appraisal of teacher induction. *Australian Journal of Teacher Education, 41*(2), 16–31. http://doi.org/10.14221/ajte.2016v41n2.2

Amadeo, K., & Boyle, M. J. (2021). What is human capital? *The Balance*. www.thebalance.com/human-capital-definition-examples-impact-4173516

Beaver, J. K., & Weinbaum, E. H. (2012). Measuring school capacity, maximizing school improvement. *CPRE Policy Briefs*. https://repository.upenn.edu/cpre_policybriefs/41

Bridwell-Mitchell, E. N., & Cooc, N. (2016). The ties that bind: How social capital is forged and forfeited in teacher communities. *Educational Researcher, 45*(1), 7–17. https://doi.org/10.3102/0013189X16632191

Carr, M., Holmes, W., & Flynn, K. (2017). Using mentoring, coaching, and self-mentoring to support educators. *Cleaning House, 90*(4), 116–124. https://doi.org/10.1080/00098655.2017.1316624

Claridge, T. (2019). Understanding the impact of your social capital. *Social Capital Research*. www.socialcapitalresearch.com/understanding-the-impact-of-your-social-capital/

Coleman, J. S. (1988). Social capital in the creation of human capital. *American Journal of Sociology, 94*, S95–S120. https://doi.org/10.1086/228943

Crocker, R. (2006). *Skills and knowledge for Canada's future: Seven perspectives towards an integrated approach to human capital development*. Canadian Policy Research Networks, Inc.

DeCesare, D., Workman, S., & McClelland, A. (2016). *How do school districts mentor new teachers?* National Center for Education Evaluation and Regional Assistance. http://ies.ed.gov/ncee/edlabs/projects/project.asp?projectID=4497

Drago-Severson, E., & Blum-DeStefano, J. (2014). Leadership for transformational learning: A developmental approach to supporting leaders' thinking and practice. *Journal of Research on Leadership Education*, *9*(2), 113–141. https://doi.org/10.1177/1942775114527082

Education Reform. (2013). *Capacity*. www.edglossary.org/capacity/

Feiman-Nemser, S., Schwille, S., Carver, C., & Yusko, B. (1999). *A conceptual review of literature on new teacher induction*. National Partnership for Excellence and Accountability in Teaching.

Fenwick, A. (2011). The first three years: Experiences of early career teachers. *Teachers & Teaching*, *17*(3), 325–343. https://doi.org/10.108 0/13540602.2011.554707

Gamborg, L., Webb, A. W., Smith, A., & Baumgartner J. J. (2018). Understanding self-efficacy of novice teachers during induction. *Research Issues in Contemporary Education*, *3*(2), 16–26. ISSN: 2690-9251

Goldin, C. (2001). The human-capital century and American leadership: Virtues of the past. *The Journal of Economic History*, *61*(2), 263–292. www.jstor.org/stable/2698021

Goldstein, D. (2014). *The teacher wars: A history of America's most embattled profession*. Anchor Books.

Gordon, E., Trygstad, P., Pasley, J., & Banilower, E. (2016). *How teachers develop social capital: Illustrative cases from the Knowles Science Teaching Foundation*. Knowles Science Teaching Foundation. https://knowlesteachers.org/wp-content/uploads/2017/11/How-Teachers-Develop-Social-Capital-ER042016-02-1.pdf

Hangül, Ş., & Şentürk, İ. (2019). Analyzing teachers' interactions through social network analysis: A multi-case study of three schools in Van, Turkey. *New Waves-Educational Research and Development Journal*, *22*(2), 16–36.

Hansen, M. (2013). Investigating the role of human resources in school turnaround: A decomposition of improving schools in two states. *Working paper 89*. National Center for Analysis of Longitudinal Data in Education Research.

Hanushek, E. A. (1989). The impact of differential expenditures on school performance. *Educational Researcher, 18*(4), 45–62. https://doi.org/10.3102/0013189X018004045

Hargreaves, A., & Fullan, M. (2012). *Professional capital: Transforming teaching in every school*. Teachers College Press.

Hatch, T. (2015). Connections, coherence, and common understanding in the common core. In J. A. Supovitz, & J. P. Spillane (Eds.), *Challenging standards: Navigating conflict and building capacity in the era of the common core* (pp. 103–111). Rowman & Littlefield.

Hirsh, S. (2010). Collective responsibility makes all teachers the best. *Teachers Teaching Teachers, 6*(1), 4–5. https://learningforward.org/wp-content/uploads/2010/09/collective-responsibility.pdf

Hong, Y., & Matsko, K. (2019). Looking inside and outside of mentoring: Effects on new teachers' organizational commitment. *American Educational Research Journal, 56*(6), 2368–2497. https://doi.org/10.3102/0002831219843657

Hudson, P. (2012). How can schools support beginning teachers? A call for timely induction and mentoring for effective teaching. *Australian Journal of Teacher Education, 37*(7), 71–82. http://doi.org/10.14221/ajte.2012v37n7.1

Ingersoll, R. M. (2018). Richard Ingersoll updates landmark study of the American teaching force, now covering 3 decades. *Penn GSE* [Press Releases]. www.gse.upenn.edu/news/press-releases/richard-ingersoll-updates-landmark-study-american-teaching-force-now-covering-3

Katzenmeyer, M., & Moller, G. (2009). *Awakening the sleeping giant: Helping teachers develop as leaders* (2nd ed.). Corwin Press.

Killion, J., Harrison, C., Colton, A., Bryan, C., Delehant, A., & Cooke, D. (2016). *A systemic approach to elevating teacher leadership*. Leaning Forward.

King Rice, J., & Malen, B. (2003). The human costs of education reform: The case of school reconstitution. *Educational Administration Quarterly, 39*(5), 635–666. https://doi.org/10.1177/0013161X03257298.

Lanoue, P. D., & Zepeda, S. J. (2018). *The emerging work of today's super-intendent: Leading schools and communities to educate all children*. Rowman & Littlefield.

Leana, C., & Pil, F. (2006). Social capital and organizational performance: Evidence from urban public schools. *Organization Science, 17*(3), 353–366. https://doi.org/10.1287/orsc.1060.0191

Lee, V. E., & Smith, J. B. (1996). Collective responsibility for learning and its effects on gains in achievement for early secondary school students. *American Journal of Education, 104*(2), 103–147. https://doi.org/10.1086/444122

Lin, N. (2001). *Social capital: A theory of social structure and action*. Cambridge University Press.

Louis, K. S., Mayrowetz, D., Murphy, J. F., & Smylie, M. (2013). Making sense of distributed leadership: How secondary school educators look at job redesign. *International Journal of Educational Leadership and Management, 1*(1) 33–68. https://doi.org/10.4471/ijelm.2013.02

Massachusetts Department of Elementary and Secondary Education. (2016). *Research on effective practices for school turnaround*. www.doe.mass.edu/turnaround/howitworks/turnaround-practices-508.pdf

Mokyr, J. (2004). *The gifts of Athena: Historical origins of the knowledge economy*. Princeton University Press.

Moolenaar, N. M., & Sleegers, P. J. C. (2015). The networked principal: Examining principals' social relationships and transformational leadership in school and district networks. *Journal of Educational Administration, 53*(1), 8–39. https://doi.org/10.1108/JEA-02-2014-0031

Moolenaar, N. M., Sleegers, P. J. C., & Daly, A. J. (2012). Teaming up: Linking collaboration networks, collective efficacy, and student achievement. *Teaching and Teacher Education, 28*(2), 251–262. https://doi.org/10.1016/j.tate.2011.10.001

Myung, J., Martinez, K., & Nordstrum, L. (2013). *A human capital frame-work for a stronger teacher workforce*. Carnegie Foundation for the Advancement of Teaching.

Neumerski, C. M. (2013). Rethinking instructional leadership, a review: What do we know about principal, teacher, and coach instructional lead-ership, and where should we go from here? *Educational Administration Quarterly, 49*(2), 310–347. doi.org/10.1177/0013161X12456700

Nguyen, T. D., & Hunter, S. (2018). Towards an understanding of dynamics among teachers, teacher leaders, and administrators in a teacher-led school reform. *Journal of Educational Change, 19*(4), 539–565. https://doi.org/10.1007/s10833-017-9316-x

No Child Left Behind Act of 2002, Pub. L. 107–110, 115 Stat. 1425, as amended by 20 U.S.C. § 6301.

Penuel, W. R., Riel, M., Joshi, A., Pearlman, L., Kim, C. M., & Frank, K. A. (2010). The alignment of the informal and formal organizational supports for reform: Implications for improving teaching in schools. *Educational Administration Quarterly, 46*(1), 57–95. https://doi.org/10.1177/1094670509353180

Penuel, W. R., Riel, M., Krause, A. E., & Frank, K. A. (2009). Analyzing teachers' professional interactions in a school as social capital: A social network approach. *Teachers College Record, 111*(1), 124–163. www.tcrecord.org

Ronfeldt, M., & McQueen, K. (2017). Does new teacher induction really improve retention? *Journal of Teacher Education, 68*(4), 394-410. https://doi.org/10.1177/0022487117702583

Saunders, M., Alcantara, V., Cervantes, L., Del Razo, J., López, R., & Perez, W. (2017). *Getting to teacher ownership: How schools are creating meaningful change; Executive summary.* Brown University, Annenberg Institute for School Reform. www.annenberginstitute.org/publications/getting-teacher-ownership-how-schools-are-creating-meaningful-change

Solution Tree. (2018). *Creating consensus for a culture of collective responsibility.* https://cloudfront-s3.solutiontree.com/pdfs/Reproducibles_TARTI/creatingconsensusforacultureofcollectiveresponsibility.pdf

Spillane, J. P. (2012). *Distributed leadership.* Jossey-Bass.

Srinivasan, L., & Archer, J. (2018). From fragmentation to coherence: How more integrative ways of thinking could accelerate improvement and progress toward equity in education. *Carnegie Corporation of New York.* https://media.carnegie.org/filer_public/16/59/16592342-9aa0-4b1a-90fc-6242d1b09197/from_fragmentation_to_coherence_nov2018.pdf

Srivastava, K., & Das, R. C. (2015). Human capital management: Economics of psychological perspective. *Industrial Psychiatry Journal, 24*(2), 115. https://doi.org/10.4103%2F0972-6748.181717

Sutcher, L., Darling-Hammond, L., & Carver-Thomas, D. (2019). Understanding teacher shortages: An analysis of teacher supply and demand in the United States. *Education Policy Analysis Archives, 27*(35), 3–28. http://doi.org/10.14507/epaa.27.3696

U.S. Department of Education. (2009). *Race to the Top Program: Executive summary*. U.S. Department of Education. www2.ed.gov/programs/racetothetop/index.html

Warford, M. (2011). The zone of proximal teacher development. *Teaching and Teacher Education, 27*(2), 252–258. https://doi.org/10.1016/j.tate.2010.08.008

Wenner, J. A., & Campbell, T. (2017). The theoretical and empirical basis of teacher leadership: A review of the literature. *Review of Educational Research, 87*(1), 134–171. https://doi.org/10.3102/0034654316653478

York-Barr, J., & Duke, K. (2004). What do we know about teacher leadership? Findings from two decades of scholarship. *Review of Educational Research, 74*(3), 255–316. https://doi.org/10.3102/00346543074003255

Zepeda, S. J. (Ed.). (2018). *Making learning job-embedded: Cases from the field of instructional leadership*. Rowman & Littlefield.

Zepeda, S. J., Derrington, M. L., & Lanoue, P. D. (2021). *Developing the organizational culture of the central office: Collaboration, connectivity, and coherence*. Routledge.

Zepeda, S. J., Parylo, O., & Klar, H. W. (2017). Educational leadership for teaching and learning. In D. Waite & I. Bogotch (Eds.), *International handbook of educational leadership* (pp. 227–252). John Wiley & Sons.

7 Leveraging Culture to Stabilize the School House

Examining School Culture

A progressive school district known to be out in front on education innovation and responsiveness to social issues launched a process of examining

 DOI: 10.4324/9781003222651-7

school culture; its resiliency in the midst of turbulence and change and its influence on their work moving forward. The process required every school in the district to create conversations between leaders, teachers, and staff about the key unifying elements as depicted in Figure 1.1 (see Chapter 1) to help them to create stability that has been impacted by recent events.

Using a SWOT analysis approach and the culture unifying elements to determine Strengths, Weaknesses (Vulnerabilities), Opportunities, and Threats, each school was to develop a plan on how to best rethink and develop their culture in the midst of innovation as well as how to ensure it buffers disruption to maintain stability. The plan was to include:

1. An opening narrative describing the current school culture.
2. Findings from their SWOT analysis.
3. A process using teacher voice and agency and the information from the SWOT analysis to identify areas of focus and to develop appropriate strategies.

Each plan required full approval by teachers and leaders and needed to include a timeline of implementation with a continuous review process.

Introduction

The turbulence in schools as a result of the ongoing challenges created from the COVID-19 pandemic uprooted many of the systems historic to the school experience. Walking into the school house in the morning, classes scheduled throughout the day, lunchroom and recess, and extracurricular activities were staples of school culture familiar to most and perhaps, expectations for generations moving forward.

Culture has unique qualities in every school, and these qualities establish the conditions for teachers to be effective in the classroom to ensure the best learning conditions for students. However, culture continues to be elusive and unrealized in most school improvement efforts (see Chapter 1). When schools shuttered their doors due to COVID-19, the impact of culture became visible and its characteristics open to definition. Furthermore, the impact of culture emerged as a focal point as schools responded to the many impacts of the changing conditions created through the trail of COVID-19 to the present day with the Delta variant.

The new normal for school culture is an understanding of the dynamics that change and resiliency will play as central to how education must be reshaped. While many hope schools will return to normal, it has been evident that schools will only return to a "new" normal. Furthermore, the new normal will be stabilized through an understanding of the Framework for School Culture and the interplay between unifying elements embedded under the waterline of the iceberg presented in Figure 1.1 in Chapter 1. This chapter outlines cultural turbulence and disruption and the role of leadership in navigating and building school cultures for their schools today because tomorrow is too late.

 ## Culture, Turbulence, and Disruption

School culture evolves and changes through the interactions by the people within the system. Embedded within the culture "rests on the norms of behavior, patterns of communication and the ways of working with each other, sub-groups of the culture, and the community at large" (Zepeda & Lanoue, 2021a, p. 51). In times of turbulence, there are many pivot points requiring schools and their systems to make rapid-fire decisions often with information that is tentative and changing by the hour. These pivots test the mettle of school culture. Today and moving forward, understanding the power of school culture may be the most significant asset for leaders and teachers because school culture is what can buffer disruptions that will surely erupt.

Turbulence

Turbulence comes in all shapes and levels of magnitude. Turbulence can be internal or external. Turbulence is rarely planned; however, the system's response is made with a firmer footing when a culture is ready to adapt to the movements of turbulence. In moving post-COVID-19, the impact of emerging external forces will bring tremendous pressures on the workings of schools and their cultures. There are two major types of turbulence that create either external or internal disruptions.

External Turbulence

Schools across the country have historically been tightly connected in delivering solutions to societal disruptions. Educational programming in areas such as government and democracy, emerging social issues, food and nutrition programs, mandated safety training or in delivery of health services, schools have been placed in positions to shoulder solutions to address issues and counter societal disruptions. However, with the onset and ongoing challenges of COVID-19 and now the Delta variant, required or rejected curriculum, and an influx of misinformation, schools are continuing to be exposed to turbulence never before experienced. The types of external turbulence could include, for example:

- States want to write curriculum to exclude historical events.

- Conversations around race and equity villainize critical race theory.

- The use of social media and news outlets to excite the public through often spread mis-information.

- The current environment of "prove me wrong," serving to polarize segments of the community.

- Mask mandates, limits on virtual learning opportunities, and seat-time requirements counted through the number of days for credit—all move attention away from students.

- Community unrest at public board of education meetings and divisiveness of communities serve to interfere with established governance structures.

- Division of responsibilities between schools and their parents as seen with mask mandates and safety, working parents whose children must be shuttered because of COVID-19.

- Future landscapes of vaccinations have divided communities with mudslinging between "anti-vaxers" and those who embrace personal and community safety.

- Students with special needs, least restrictive learning environments and mask requirements moving into court cases.

- Teacher walk-outs and protests; protests by parents at board of education meetings; and other public displays that interrupt schools and systems from focusing on the core mission of educating students.

This list could continue but suffice to say, schools are microcosms of their communities, and the tenor of the times can infiltrate the work schools need to engage on behalf of the children whose parents have entrusted them to its care.

The turbulence caused by the current political environment has surfaced with a vengeance by creating high levels of toxicity and divisiveness impacting the work of teachers, leaders, and local school boards. In fact, today, schools are more in the political foray than ever before and are now a focal point in the current political culture war. Groves (2021) shared:

> Local school boards around the country are increasingly becoming cauldrons of anger and political division, boiling with disputes over such issues as COVID-19 mask rules, the treatment of transgender students, and how to teach the history of racism and slavery in America.
>
> (para. 1)

These political forces will continuously impact school culture through mandates that are normally based on decisions discussed and approved at the local level.

Whether the decision to wear masks for the safety of students and teachers or legislative curricular mandates, the voice of communities and their teachers have until recently been muted and discarded. In a recent interview with Randi Weingarten, president of the American Federation of Teachers, Smith (2021) reports that the political culture war is "about constant destabilization, creating anger, exploiting the anxiety that people have right now," and she further explained that "It is also kind of rooted in the destabilization of the institutions in America that have, you know, long been used to unify the country. Like great neighborhood public schools" (para. 28).

The interactions of the external environment by parents, political groups, and state and federal mandates have presented new influences on how schools function to the point of testing the unifying elements (such as autonomy, collective efficacy, professional engagement, etc.) that work to create a school culture as depicted in Figure 1.1 (Chapter 1). In moving forward, it is evident that external disruptions will be ongoing and will critically influence school leaders on the importance of school culture in the midst of change. With this understanding, it is clear that school culture must be leveraged to stabilize the turbulence faced by the school house and the leaders who must be calm before, during, and after the proverbial storms.

Internal Turbulence

School leaders have limited control over the external influences on school culture. Knowledge about the external factors helps to minimize the impact of them on the internal risks and allows leaders and teachers to create clarity, confidence, and trust within the system. Leading a positive school culture is not an add-on to improving schools but rather culture is the foundation from which schools need to operate and improve. Important for leaders is understanding the value of culture and what factors, positive and negative influence its development as found in the unifying elements under the waterline in the iceberg as depicted in Figure 1.1 in Chapter 1.

To lead culture shifts, school leaders must first understand their schools, its history, its successes, its challenges, and its influencers within the system. Leaders must identify the positive aspects of culture such as teacher empowerment and autonomy, care and support, sense of belonging, efficacy and professional engagement, all the while understanding the warning signs of a negative culture (see Chapter 3 for discussion about positive and negative school culture). Warning signs of a negative culture that leaders should look for include:

- lack of direction and sense of purpose;
- poor relations between staff, students, and parents;
- a focus on rules rather than mission;
- blaming students for poor performance;
- lack of open and honest conversations;
- teachers who are more concerned over self-interest rather than group interest;
- employing a punishment mentality vs. reward mentality;
- allowing small groups to control the conversations and outcomes;
- poor communication and information breakdowns; and
- lack of risk-taking.

(Epitropoulos, 2019)

When new initiatives are introduced, it is important for leaders to understand their culture. Often and especially during national movements for school reform, initiatives never reached their potential effectiveness or widespread application due to a conflict with existing cultural norms and professional expectations.

Digging deeper, culture is more than implementing random strategies. Katzenbach et al. (2012) underscore, "A strategy that is at odds with an organization's culture is doomed. Culture trumps strategy every time" (Katzenbach et al., 2012, para. 11). Strategies must be embedded and supported by the culture. Understanding culture and alignment to practice remains primary for long-term success with existing practices or when implementing new practices.

Critical to understanding culture is realizing that culture is also personal and is built on trust to the extent that "Whatever matters to human beings, trust is the atmosphere in which it thrives" (Moses, 2019, para. 3). Toxic cultures emerge quickly when leaders lack empathy and fail to develop relationships within the system (see Chapter 3).

Personal and Professional Turbulence

Teachers and school leaders are influenced greatly by the culture in which they work and from this affiliation, leaders create a lens that determines how they see themselves and others. The culture lens is shaped and influenced by this world view and further shaped by and through relationships and responsibility for the people in the school. Culture has a personal effect, and culture also influences relationships with others and the personal and professional events associated with schools. According to Raeff (2010), culture influences:

- relationships;
- traits such as humility, self-esteem, politeness, and assertiveness;
- perceptions of hardship and how leaders feel about relying on others;
- how success is defined and whether certain types of individual and group achievements are valued and promoted; and,
- how and whether feelings are expressed publicly or privately.

Table 7.1 Developing Shared Meanings

Psychological and Social Influences	That Lead To . . .
Identity	A sense of who people are as a group.
Commitment	A sense of seeing beyond self-interest.
Behavioral standards	The acknowledgment and ability to follow unwritten rules.
Social control and social stability	The willingness to share and embrace cultural values, beliefs, and practices.

Source: Adapted from Kaplan and Owings (2013)

Moreover, school culture establishes a psychological and social environment that influences and strengthens the development of shared meanings that the school embraces as identified in Table 7.1.

These influences serve to strengthen a sense of belonging and morale among the members of the school (see Chapter 2).

When cultures are in a state of turbulence, it creates a personal and professional imbalance with a range of effects. Relationships within schools become strained while the commitment levels and behavioral expectations disrupt social patterns and the ways in which individuals interact and respond. As an example, the disruption caused by the requirement of masks in schools due to COVID-19 is a stark example of personal and professional turbulence that is rippling across all schools in the country. School culture emanates from people and their relationship to each other. Personal and professional turbulence often has long term implications for the working relationships critical to a positive culture and effective working conditions.

Whether turbulence is external or internal or personal and professional, the disruptions can chip away at morale, impact workplace conditions (see Chapter 2), and have the potential to create toxic conditions (see Chapter 3). All of these conditions can lead to consequences that erode even the healthiest and most positive school cultures. For leaders, understanding how culture is impacted by internal and external disruptions and recognizing the kinds of disruptions that can occur will be pivotal in moving forward from the conditions that can play havoc within the schoolhouse. With these understandings, leaders and teachers are better able to be ready for whatever comes next.

Leading Culture

Understanding Culture

1. Schools are microcosms of their community and external turbulence will invariably impact school culture.

2. Internal turbulence is buffered when leaders have established confidence and trust with school staff.

3. Turbulence, regardless of whether the disruption originates inside or outside the school building, may have personal and professional impact on staff.

Leveraging the Power of Culture

1. Identify the most salient external factors that currently disrupt your teachers' professional work and personal well-being.

2. Reflect on how and when to facilitate conversations with staff to identify the sources of internal turbulence.

3. To what degree does your school culture provide outlets for staff to seek help in dealing with personal and professional turbulence and disruptions?

Readying for Tomorrow Through Culture

Through the recent turbulence felt by schools resulting from internal and external disruptions, leaders are now in an urgent yet unique position to ensure schools are and remain stable. The many dynamics impacting schools from the injection of politics in educational decisions to a dichotomy of instructional delivery—in school vs. virtual school—are requiring leaders to focus on school culture. However, leaders must also be aware that a stable culture is one that is not static, but one that evolves as internal and external factors influence its unifying elements (see Chapter 1, Figure 1.1.).

A stable culture is not impenetrable from internal or external disruptions. However, a stable culture is able to buffer disruption and support positive change and innovation. School leaders are now in a unique position to leverage the power of school culture in new ways to support teachers through disruptions while initiating new practices to improve student achievement.

Stable school cultures, especially during times of continuous change, are ones that are able to not only stabilize disruptions but also they are able to navigate new aspects of culture to support change. While a stable culture can often be seen as static and resistant to change and innovation, a stable culture can also lend itself to successful change. To the point, organizations with a relatively high degree of stability in their culture, often created through bureaucracy and hierarchy, may be able to effectively navigate change with leader controls (Janka et al., 2020).

A healthy culture is not built on rigid control and hierarchical structures that chip away at morale. As examined in Chapter 3, leaders who create healthy school cultures understand that school culture is dynamic and continuously shifting through school transformation and adaptation in response to internal and external turbulence. Furthermore, leaders with a culture vision understand how it supports the needs of teachers and their readiness to handle change.

Leading Through Cultural Turbulence

While school leaders have historically responded to internal and external turbulence, their ability to lead cultural adaptation will now be a necessity. In this time of rapid social turbulence, school leaders will need to recognize that turbulence often signals change. Change—planned or unplanned—signals a certain amount of turbulence. School culture is now more than ever before foundational to buffering unneeded change while readying for positive cultural adaptations.

Leaders must be able to recognize cultural turbulence and its potential impact. They are pivotal as school cultures evolve and are readied for change associated with turbulence. From a culture lens, Reeves (2006) suggests that leaders are effective in leading culture through change by clarifying what is not going to change which also acknowledges accomplishments and what works well. Leaders who can navigate turbulence through a cultural lens maintain a high level of trust while maintaining the political capital they need. Leaders who create a school culture that is stable and responsive are deliberate and knowledgeable about the unifying elements (Chapter 1) within their school's culture.

One of the most significant disruptions in public education occurred when schools shut their doors to in-person learning as a result of COVID-19 pandemic. The turbulence when schools moved to a virtual environment revealed much about the impact of school culture. When teachers moved to virtual environments, the daily in-school rituals and routines, norms, and beliefs about their culture changed dramatically. Leaders needed to rethink not only instructional delivery but also imagine a drastically different school culture that now resided outside of the school walls.

What did we learn about culture from the COVID-19 pandemic? We learned that in times of turbulence, leaders need to rethink how they lead through disruption knowing that the culture will change. Culture emanates from relationships between those within the school, and leaders must engage in supporting human processes in addition to the mechanics of school operations. According to Groysberg et al. (2021), "Conversations are the best way to get leaders and employees back into the practice of relating to one another in person" (para. 4).

For leaders, creating conversations during turbulent times is intentional. Groysberg et al. (2021) suggests that leaders use a framework for creating critical conversation to move organizations through cultural disruptions. Drawing from this work, Table 7.2 offers an adapted framework including the elements that can support leaders to focus their conversations. These strategies can help understand and make sense of disturbances that can test the mettle of a school culture.

Table 7.2 Creating Critical Conversations

Elements and Guiding Questions	Strategies
Intimacy How do leaders relate to employees?	• Acknowledge in a timely manner facts with honesty and transparency. • Acknowledge feelings recognizing the strain felt with uncertainty. • As a way to break the ice and show vulnerability, leaders model by going first in sharing their feelings. • Teachers, staff, and others are given opportunities to share their feelings and reactions.

(Continued)

Table 7.2 (Continued)

Elements and Guiding Questions	Strategies
Interactivity How do leaders use communication channels?	• Check for psychological feelings of safety while teachers and staff share honest opinions and ideas. • Recap conversation to affirm active listening.
Inclusion How do leaders organize content?	• Connect Conversations to school priorities, school improvement goals, and the vision and mission of the school and system. • Create social identity and a sense of belonging based on shared values, norms, and habits. • Stay connected and include the community. • Recognize and develop internal expertise, teacher leadership, and support structures.
Intentionality How do leaders convey strategy?	• Understand and have clarity in all communications with teachers and staff. • Structure and share conversation topics in advance to give teachers and staff and community members the opportunity to collect thoughts. • Connect conversations to actions.
Follow-up Mechanisms How do leaders follow-up on conversations?	• Conversations rarely end; they continue for as long as necessary; therefore, leaders follow-up with the necessary supports that bubble up during conversations. • Engage others with follow-up on conversation content.

Source: Adapted from Groysberg et al. (2021)

A caveat is offered. The elements and guiding questions can be used more broadly to frame conversations in times of "zero" turbulence in schools. In other words, conversations are at the heart of the interactions that leaders and teachers engage in as daily habits.

The most effective approach to leading through turbulence is understanding that "people" create and change their culture. A focus on the "then" well before crisis best prepares and positions leaders to lead through disruption. Zepeda and Lanoue (2021a) report the work of Dr. Susan Stancil, former principal of Dove Creek Elementary School (Oconee County, Ga) that "the foundation of culture and relationships must be in place so your school can withstand any turbulence that disrupts schools from serving students and families" (p. 92).

Stabilizing Through Unifying Elements

In Chapter 1, the iceberg figure is presented as a graphic representation of the dynamics of school culture. Before the waterline are a grouping of unifying elements that are in constant motion, influencing the school culture. To stabilize the culture, leaders must redirect their focus on understanding how these unifying elements affect their school's culture. We cannot ignore culture and just move along—culture is the most valuable asset a school can have as they face change and disruptions. Schools can thrive amid disruption if culture is realized as the great buffer. While disruption can be a recipe for a perfect disaster, it can also create opportunities when stable and responsive.

Leading through culture requires leaders to understand their current culture and to create a culture vision (Chapter 3). Reflection through a culture lens using key culture questions will help leaders understand their culture and enable them to effectively lead through disruption, and readying to make necessary changes. Table 7.3 looks at the unifying elements of culture as depicted in the iceberg (Chapter 1, Figure 1.1) to help leaders frame questions related to stabilizing a school culture.

Table 7.3 Culture Unifying Elements—Critical Questions Bring Clarity

Unifying Elements	Critical Questions
Sense of Belonging [see Chapter 1]	How do I support teachers in feeling a part of the school and that they are valued for the uniqueness they bring?
Support, Care, and Safety [see Chapter 5]	How do colleagues support each other both personally and professionally?
Empowerment and Autonomy [see Chapters 1 and 2]	How are teachers supported in making decisions about their classroom, and are they involved in schoolwide decision-making processes?

(Continued)

Table 7.3 (Continued)

Unifying Elements	Critical Questions
Collaboration [see Chapter 5]	How do teachers collaborate on lesson design, instructional delivery, and developing needed professional learning?
Professional Engagement [see Chapter 5 and 6]	How do teachers and leaders engage professionally to improve practices and model lifelong learning?
Self-Efficacy [see Chapter 1 and 3]	How do you know if teachers hold the belief that they can be successful and that school improvement stems from believing that collective voices and actions lead to success?
Collective Efficacy [see Chapter 1]	How do teachers hold a shared belief that they can have a positive impact on student achievement?
Collective Ownership and Responsibility [see Chapters 1 through 6]	In what ways do teachers *together* assume mutual ownership for their decisions and the resulting outcomes?
Teacher Voice and Teacher Agency [see Chapters 1 through 6]	In what ways does teacher voice and their actions create opportunities for improving schools differently from past practices predicated on top-down leadership approaches?

Departing from the traditional definition of cultural stability is understanding that stable cultures shift in this view, and that change is not a knee-jerk reaction. Important for leaders today, is:

- understanding culture's unifying elements and embracing the concept that stable cultures need to shift and move knowing that returning to the status quo is not always the best option;

- realizing that the unifying elements are not static—there is an ebb and flow that changes as dynamics within the school shift;

- recognizing that in their totality, these unifying elements can be harnessed that promotes collective responsibility and action; and,

- accepting that a positive school culture is built through teacher agency and voice. Without teacher voice and agency, it is unlikely that a school culture can evolve to sustain disruption and turbulence. In other words, a school culture is only as positive as its teachers' abilities to own and act on their beliefs, knowledge, and expertise they bring to the school.

Developing culture to help stabilize school disruption is not a one-time event but rather an ongoing process requiring focus, attention, and action. Leading a stable culture through a cultural lens requires leaders to:

1. Identify the school's influences—the existing assumptions, norms, values, and organizational rules.

2. Make public how well the underlying norms, assumptions, and practices support—or hinder—student learning.

3. Question and replace outdated or misaligned assumptions and practices that directly or indirectly help improve all students' achievement.

4. Continually monitor, assess, and adjust the outcomes of changed behaviors as a result of culture shifts.

(Kaplan & Owings, 2013)

Leading with a cultural vision requires leaders to go beyond their individual views of culture and requires an understanding of the complexities of culture through the multiple lenses of those within the system. The subcultures within schools have a significant impact on the unifying elements that are foundational to school culture.

Impact of Subcultures

Leading through a culture lens is complex and therefore cannot be oversimplified by discussing only a single culture within a school. Every school has subcultures that have emerged over time through varying roles within the school and relationships of those who work in the system. School culture is influenced by many stakeholders other than teachers to include students, parents, administration, staff, and community members. Also, teacher subcultures can be found in groups with relationships developed from their teaching experience, years in the school, area of expertise, and educational background. Often these subcultures may not fully share the values and norms of the school culture causing cultural turbulence. When leaders understand their subcultures, they are better positioned to create cultural responsiveness and stability.

In readying school culture, responding to a single culture or a culture through a single lens will not provide leaders with the culture view they need. Every school has a subculture and every school's subculture can influence the school's culture. As leaders understand their culture and related subcultures they should:

1. Identify where subcultures exist and understand their influence.

2. Use multiple information points, both formal and informal to assess levels of subculture influence.

3. Approach culture conversations starting with the whole, then part, then whole—when communicating to a subculture, connect the message with the "whole" organization's culture.

4. Address dysfunction as subcultures can veer from the organization and even turn into a counterculture.

5. Engage the subcultures by including them in school wide conversations, planning, and in seeking solutions to existing problems.

(Adapted from Emerson, 2018)

While culture is seen as a whole, understanding and influencing subcultures is a critical aspect of stabilizing culture in the midst of disruption and change. Influencing cultures is a human endeavor requiring inclusive human processes that build a sense of belonging, show care, and create an environment of trust (see Chapter 4).

Understanding and leveraging the power of school culture may likely be the greatest asset for school leaders in navigating disruption and creating positive change to improve student achievement. The new school house, post-COVID-19 and its trailing disruptions will continually look different. This new look and sound of disruption will require new thinking on supporting a positive school culture where the school house may not have physical boundaries or daily class schedules.

Leading Culture

Understanding Culture

1. School culture will evolve, especially during times of cultural turbulence; therefore, leaders must be intentional about clarifying for teachers what is and is not going to change.

2. Efforts to understand and stabilize school culture should be guided through the unifying elements (see Table 7.3).

3. Leaders must identify and be responsive to the subcultures in the building that exist within the broader school culture.

Leveraging the Power of Culture

1. In leading culture through change, reflect on how to leverage trust and political capital to protect what is working well but address areas in need of improvement.

2. How do you create the time and space for critical conversations to move your school through cultural disruptions (see Table 7.2)?

3. What relevant subcultures exist within your school building and how do you determine their degree of influence?

Culture in the New School House

The role of culture moving forward, especially given the dynamics created by COVID-19 and political, social, and racial unrest has launched critical conversations about school culture. School culture, often thought as an afterthought to building school morale, is now center in seeking solutions to navigate future disruptions. For school leaders, deciding if culture creates stability during turbulence or does turbulence change the culture is no different than what came first—the chicken or the egg? In either of these positions, the major shift is that culture will be ever present as schools embark on new foundational changes in instructional delivery and social emotional support for students and teachers.

School Culture Expanded

Schools across the country have historically been tightly connected in delivering solutions to societal disruptions. Schools have been placed in positions to shoulder solutions to address issues and counter societal disruptions through educational programming in areas such as:

- emerging social issues;
- food and nutrition programs;
- mandated safety training;
- delivery of health services; and,
- restorative justice.

The list of services and programs are almost unlimited.

With the onset and ongoing challenges of COVID-19 and its variants, schools are now in a position like no other period in history. Schools can no longer function as business as in the past if they are to shoulder and buffer the pressures from growing turbulence. As school districts navigate their path through changing times, school and community culture will have a significant influence on critical decisions on school programs. The norms and values of a school's culture will no longer be confined or influenced by what occurs only within the school house walls. Decisions are now made as much around community culture as they are school culture. This expansion of culture outside the school boundaries lends itself to a new set of cultural influences previously viewed as external.

This shift in cultural boundaries presents new challenges for school leaders and teachers to redefine their culture far differently than previously before which may present new opportunities. Siegel (2020) suggests that the recent events can have a dramatic yet positive impact on school cultures given that "Transformation is survival from all points of view. If we properly use this moment for the better, it could mean improved education for more students" (para. 18). Important for leaders and teachers is to believe they can move forward in creating new conversations about culture—its norms and values—even in the midst of turbulence. Moving forward through new conversations can lead to a culture with reimagined opportunities to address the achievement of all students.

Creating an inclusive new culture will not be an easy venture for school leaders. While school culture has expanded outside the traditional schools' walls and presented new opportunities, the cultural turbulence normally viewed as external factors is now turbulence within the school culture. School cultures are now evolving through a multitude of social and political issues with little internal controls. Issues on whether to require masks, require COVID-19 testing, and the options for virtual learning models are now pivot points and have become part of the fabric of school culture evolution. Embedded in these larger culture sets are differences in ideologies, beliefs, and most recently, ideologies amplified and polarized by intense political divisions.

Leaders will need to contend with not only their school's culture but emerging community cultures as they navigate tensions between them. Inherent in these tensions are new pressures to reshape schools in how they deliver instructions—in school or virtual, the restrictions on curriculum, and teacher autonomy through political action. Navigating different views combined with social and political turbulence requires an understanding of the tensions between the culture within their schools and the culture within their communities.

Culture Tensions

The current divisions in beliefs and political views are creating increasing tensions in the schoolhouse and their communities across the country. The issues that at one time would produce some level of disruption at the district or state level are now new for schools. However, the recent culture wars have expanded beyond local and state turbulence to all-out national movements that have even become violent with physical and threatening altercations. These tensions are tearing at the culture of America's public education similar to the current turbulence around the ideology of being an American. According to Mervosh and Heyward (2021):

> the two biggest divides in schools today are also highly volatile because they challenge fundamental narratives of what it means to be an American. As an example, the debate over mask mandates puts two values into conflict, collective responsibility versus personal liberty.
>
> (para. 19)

There are many tensions that schools experience, including issues never-before experienced.

Mask mandates and vaccine requirements have created intense disruption in schools as districts contend with internal responses to mandated masks and vaccines while juggling parental pushback often driven by political divisions. In many states, political stances enacted through state policy mandates such as no masks requirements have led to districts disregarding these mandates at the risk of losing funding. The division is further seen between state and federal control as federal funds have been allocated to provide federal dollars to supplement this loss of state dollars.

Requiring vaccines for adults is resulting in teacher resignations across the country and has received much pushback with districts often seeking alternatives to those who refuse to be vaccinated by requiring COVID-19 testing. Recent state legislation to require vaccinations both for teachers and students has created intense pushback to the point of parents seeking a variety of ways to create exemptions for either health or religious reasons.

The virtual school and in-school tensions has also created culture wars between parents and school leaders to the level of political wrangling leading to state mandates for in school instruction tied to state funding. With a level of irony, virtual schools had gained momentum across the country pre-COVID-19 with many state departments of education offering virtual learning as an option. Now post-COVID-19, states are limiting the number of students who can enroll in a virtual program even though they are the ones offering it.

However, the positioning of in-school vs. virtual school is complex and more so now that it is embedded in political ideologies, likely no different than the heated conversations regarding public schools versus private charter schools. Virtual school models of education have gained momentum both in the K-12 sector as well as in colleges and universities with many college students taking at least one course online while on campus. Virtual instructional models challenge the many standard school conventions of in-school learning and have created a significant divide on how schools should be designed.

While incredible work has been done by teachers when moving to full virtual environments, the personal contact and wellbeing of students remains a critical question especially with the recent increase in the social trauma students bring with them to school. However, even with the differences in delivery, the virtual or in-school questions should not require a yes or no response. Opportunities for students to access learning via in-school or virtual should be available—in whole or in part. In other words, to meet the needs of students requires degrees of freedom of choice.

Curricular decisions have historically caused disturbances either at the school district or state level usually through the adoption of curricular materials or textbooks. Historically, there have been controversies over what students learn in schools as it shapes their thinking, national and world view, and lays ideological foundations. Shaping a national, state, or local culture emerges from what students learn in school. The inherent tensions for school leaders and teachers are whether the curriculum reflects what they want students to know or does the curriculum reflect the wishes of their community and state.

While individual states have the primary decisions over education, local school boards have authority as well including curricular adoptions. Furthermore, the federal government influences curriculum decisions by linking federal resources to curricular decisions. While the historic processes typically approved what curriculum was to be used by teachers, an emerging narrative is gaining to legislate what you cannot teach and requiring parent permission of what to teach. As an example, legislative movements are now focusing on having teachers post lesson plans for parent review and approval in advance of the lesson—being decried by teachers as a blatant assault on their integrity and professionalism (Khaled, 2021). These tensions are creating cultural controversy and divisions, fueled by politics especially around key issues of equity and in the teaching of American history.

These divisions have now created mandates of what you cannot teach such as material from the 1619 project which reframes the country's origins around the arrival of the first enslaved Africans in Virginia. Critical Race Theory (CRT), though not fully understood, is banned in many states due mainly to the fear of erosion of patriotism by presenting a different version of American history (Waxman, 2020). Similarly, CRT recognizes that racism is not a bygone relic of the past but instead acknowledges that the legacy of slavery, segregation, and the imposition of second-class citizenship on Black Americans and other people of color continue to permeate society and the schools in which children are educated.

The intensity of the culture wars has reached new levels with school leaders being consumed by disturbances that distract, leaving little time to focus on improving students' achievement. The disruption between community, parents, and schools has reached historic levels as school board officials, school leaders, teachers, and parents are experiencing verbal and physical threats for wanting masks and vaccines. Often, these threats are resulting in physical violence. The National School Boards Association (NSBA) has responded to this violence by requesting that President Biden enact legislation calling for these threats to be considered domestic terrorism (NSBA, 2021).

With the loss of face-to-face contact with students and students with each other, teachers lost the social construct familiar in their previous environment as well as familiar behaviors. New culture norms needed to be established; however, this process takes time—time they did not have. The virtual transition was confusing as no one could refer to previous rituals and routines referred to the "way we do things around here." As leaders move forward in times of turbulence, creating a positive and responsive culture requires laser focus on the unifying elements as identified in Chapter 1 in Figure 1.1, the Framework for School Culture.

New Focus

Teachers and school leaders are desperate to leave the tensions created by the current outside politics and differing ideologies and return to a time where conversations are about learning and student wellbeing. However, returning to the past will not provide the direction nor the support needed in moving forward. While the current events have been exhausting, much has been learned about the functions of schools, its influencers, and new paths to move forward. Students and teachers must remain at the center of attention for leaders.

Regardless of the uniqueness of an in-school culture or a virtual culture, one of the emerging shifts in school priorities is focusing on the wellbeing and social emotional stability of both students and teachers. Moving forward, schools must be about creating cultures of care. According to Avera (2021), schools now need to reimagine their school culture with a focus on developing relationships, rethinking rules and procedures, and ensuring regular mental health checks. The need to build trust and develop relationships, once hidden in the midst of accountability trends, needs to now be the priority for schools.

For students, a reimagined school culture built on care and concern is needed now more than ever in the wake of COVID-19 and national uproar on policing, immigration, racial inequality, etc. Students are enduring stress, anxiety, and other issues related to their health and well-being. These issues have been amplified when COVID-19. When schools shuttered their doors, children were cut off from their interactions with peers and teachers; in many instances, support services were diminished; they faced food insecurity; and often older children had to assume different roles as their parents had to work. Children carried extra burdens.

During COVID-19, schools had to patch together supports or ratchet-up existing ones as they saw a growing need by their students. Schools and their systems began to look at social emotional learning (SEL) differently, having to acknowledge that more efforts were needed. SEL includes the efforts made by educators to develop the intrapersonal and interpersonal foundational competencies that children need to evolve into productive adults. SEL skills help children handle difficult situations, and educators play an important part in helping children learn how to care for their mental wellbeing and safety.

In a convening of policy makers, scholars, and school personnel, the National Academy of Education (2020) offered five recommendations to schools related to whole-person well-being. These recommendations suggest that systems and their schools:

1. Make the social-emotional and mental health needs of students and staff the top priority. Whole person well-being is critical to academic and life success. When returning to schooling—in whatever form—the social, mental, and emotional health of our students must be thoughtfully and methodically addressed.

2. Build social-emotional learning into the school curriculum for all students. Social and emotional skills should be embedded in instruction and tied to academic competencies.

3. Provide ongoing consultation to teachers and families on challenges that they are facing in responding to children's needs. Districts and schools should have counselors/social workers/psychologists available to help teachers and families address these needs.

4. Provide group and individual sessions with mental health personnel (counselors, social workers, school psychologists) for students experiencing distress. Equitable access to school-supported social, emotional, and mental health needs of students is necessary.

5. Determine strategies for maintaining, strengthening, and developing relationships in a virtual environment. For students returning to school virtually in the fall, teachers need to work to build, and in most cases develop, new relationships in largely unfamiliar environments. Teachers will need to build a new skill set in order to develop relationships and assist with peer relationships in virtual environments.

(p. 5)

The findings drawn by the National Academy of Education (2020) acknowledged that teachers needed support and suggested that schools and systems needed to provide professional learning as well as care and concern for teachers who would be engaging with students—online or face-to-face. The National Academy of Education elaborated:

> Regardless of the environment in which teachers will return, they will need support and professional development to navigate unfinished learning, to deliver in online or hybrid models, and to address the social and emotional strains on students as well as their own persons, families, and communities. Professional development needs to include information that appropriately considers the ages of students. It also, in online and in- person environments, needs to enable teachers and staff to screen for and identify distress and trauma, and to express patience and caring and minimize bias in interactions.
> (p. 3)

School leaders learned a new lesson about teachers and the care and support that teachers needed.

As leaders responded to the unique challenges presented by COVID-19, they knew that teaching was stressful, and that for the most part, they were ill prepared to systematically support them as the stress on teachers grew exponentially. Teachers shouldered the responsibility in navigating through extreme changes in their practices, often in isolation from their peers and with no face-to-face contact with their students. While teachers have always endured stressful conditions, the new environment surfaced a critical need requiring leaders to strategically focus on their wellbeing by providing well defined and stronger supports. According to Zepeda and Lanoue (2021b), creating new paths for teachers will require

- Rethinking schedules and teaching loads.

- Creating instructional support as teachers move back and forth between delivery environments.

- Reviewing and evaluating instructional models to make necessary modifications in practices based on experiences that support the local context.

- Engaging teachers in professional learning and then providing appropriate follow-up that could include coaching and informal classroom observations with frequent feedback and discussion.

(para. 8)

All of these efforts and more are essential because "We know that teachers want to do their very best, and it falls to leaders to provide support that enables them to engage students" (Zepeda & Lanoue, 2021b, para. 8).

Although we are still learning more about the impact of disruption on school culture, leaders must continue to make significant shifts in their practices by focusing on a culture of care and support for both students and teachers as they forge ahead building a positive learning culture within their classrooms. What leaders do impacts students.

Leading Culture

Understanding Culture
1. School culture is no longer limited to what happens inside the school walls.
2. Social and political tensions require leaders to be laser-focused on building and sustaining a positive and responsive school culture.
3. Leading through internal and external disruptions will require leaders to refocus their attention on care and support for teachers and students.

Leveraging the Power of Culture
1. How are the values inherent in your internal school culture reflected in your external strategy to support and engage the community?

2. As you navigate evolving social and political tensions, how can your focus on school culture insulate your staff from the distractions?

3. In what ways can you establish a culture of care and support for teachers and students?

 # Chapter Summary

Turbulence in schools is inevitable whether internal or external. Leaders who understand what constitutes school culture are better positioned to weather turbulence and leverage its power as an asset. Furthermore, schools are a microcosm of their communities and increasingly, the influences of community culture are requiring leaders to see beyond their school's walls. Leaders and teachers, together, must now position themselves to understand their culture and be prepared to react to the changing realities inside and outside their system.

Schools have been thrust into a broader role in society. The lines that are traditionally known to delineate *in-school* and *outside-of-school* no longer exist, placing schools in both a challenging, yet exciting position. Students need a bridge that extends the principles of school culture from the classrooms to what they experience in their homes and communities. Teachers are getting entangled in cultural clashes and need clarity as they reconcile these differences in their classrooms. Teachers also need support and care as they navigate new challenges and disruptions that take away from their focus in teaching and learning. Leaders have few options other than to focus inward on the dynamics of their culture and how creating a culture vision will help them to navigate current and future disruptions.

Leading Practices

1. *Analyzing* internal and external turbulence in your school

    a. Identify the sources of internal and external turbulence in your district/school and seek input from teacher-leaders on if and how such dynamics could be addressed to improve school culture.

2. *Developing Processes* needed to improve student and teacher well-being

   a. Develop an action plan that addresses the most salient dynamics relative to teacher or student well-being.

3. *Implementing Strategies* to promote teacher and student well-being

   a. Publicly commit to your staff ways in which you will implement and measure strategies to promote student and staff well-being (which includes measurable goals for success).

Suggested Readings

Glanz, J. (Ed.). (2021). *Crisis and pandemic leadership: Implications for meeting the needs of students, teachers, and parents.* Rowman & Littlefield.

Zacarian, D., Espino Calderon, M., & Gottlieb, M. (2021). *Beyond Crises: Overcoming linguistic and cultural inequities in communities, schools, and classrooms.* Corwin Press.

Zepeda, S. J., & Lanoue, P. D. (2021). *A leadership guide to navigating the unknown in education: New narratives amid COVID-19.* Routledge.

References

Avera, A. (2021). The pandemic lessons that will rebuild school culture. *Association for Supervision and Curriculum Development.* www.ascd.org/blogs/the-pandemic-lessons-that-will-rebuild-school-culture

Emerson, T. (2018). How to manage subcultures in your organization. *Workforce.* https://workforce.com/news/how-to-manage-subcultures-organization

Epitropoulos, A. (2019). 10 signs of a toxic school culture. *Association for Supervision and Curriculum Development.* www.ascd.org/el/articles/10-signs-of-a-toxic-school-culture

Groves, S. (2021). Tears, politics and money: School boards become battle zones. *AP News*. https://apnews.com/article/health-education-coronavirus-pandemic-school-boards-e41350b7d9e3662d279c2dad287f7009

Groysberg, B., Abrahams, R., & Baden, K. C. (2021). The pandemic conversations that leaders need to have now. *Harvard Business School*. https://hbswk.hbs.edu/item/the-pandemic-conversations-that-leaders-need-to-have-now

Janka, M., Heinicke, X., & Guenther, T. W. (2020). Beyond the "good" and "evil" of stability values in organizational culture for managerial innovation: The crucial role of management controls. *Review of Managerial Science*, *14*(6), 1363–1404. https://doi.org/10.1007/s11846-019-00338-3

Kaplan, L. S., & Owings, W. A. (2013). *Culture re-boot: Reinvigorating school culture with student outcomes*. Corwin Press.

Katzenbach, J. R., Steffen, I., & Kronley, C. (2012). Cultural change that sticks. *Harvard Business Review*. https://hbr.org/2012/07/cultural-change-that-sticks

Khaled, F. (2021). Utah teachers furious over proposal to post lesson plans in advance for parent approval. *Newsweek*. www.newsweek.com/utah-teachers-furious-over-proposal-post-lesson-plans-advance-parent-approval-1641355

Mervosh, S., & Heyward, G. (2021). The school culture wars: 'You have brought division to us.' *The New York Times*. www.nytimes.com/2021/08/18/us/schools-covid-critical-race-theory-masks-gender.html

Moses, L. (2019). How trusting relationships advance school culture and influence student achievement. *Association for Supervision and Curriculum Development*. www.ascd.org/blogs/how-trusting-relationships-advance-school-culture-and-influence-student-achievement

National Academy of Education. (2020). COVID-19 educational inequities roundtable series: Summary report. *Author*. https://naeducation.org/covid-19-educational-inequities-roundtable-series-summary-report/

National School Boards Association (NSBA). (2021). *Preclusion of further threats and violence against students and educators*. https://nsba.org/-/media/NSBA/File/nsba-letter-to-president-biden-concerning-threats-to-public-schools-and-school-board-members-92921.pdf

Raeff, C. (2010). Independence and interdependence in children's developmental experiences. *Child Development Perspectives, 4*(1), 31–36. https://doi.org/10.1111/j.1750-8606.2009.00113.x

Reeves, D. B. (2006). Leading to change: How do you change school culture? *Association for Supervision and Curriculum Development.* www.ascd.org/el/articles/how-do-you-change-school-culture

Siegel, M. (2020). 5 major shifts needed post-COVID-19 to transform education. *Government Technology.* www.govtech.com/education/k-12/five-major-shifts-needed-post-covid-19-to-transform-education.html

Smith, A. (2021). Schools become political 'battlefield' in culture wars Trump cultivated. *NBC News.* www.nbcnews.com/politics/politics-news/schools-become-political-battlefield-culture-wars-trump-cultivated-n1278257

Waxman, O. B. (2020). Trump's threat to pull funding from schools over how they teach slavery is part of a long history of politicizing American history class. *Time.* https://time.com/5889051/history-curriculum-politics/

Zepeda, S. J., & Lanoue, P. D. (2021a). *A leadership guide to navigating the unknown in education: New narratives amid COVID-19.* Routledge.

Zepeda, S. J., & Lanoue, P. D. (2021b). *Needed: Support for teachers on the COVID-19 front line.* www.routledge.com/blog/article/needed-support-for-teachers-on-the-covid-19-front-line#

It's All About Culture

DOI: 10.4324/9781003222651-8

Introduction

There is not an easy way to end a book that asks school leaders to reflect on how they work alongside teachers, staff, parents, and community members to build a positive school culture. The book might be ending, but the necessary conversations at the school-level must continue as daily practice. We are using this space to underscore and to tie together the key take-aways about school culture and to underscore the needed collaborative work of teachers and leaders to make culture the centerpiece of all efforts for continuous improvement for *all* in the schoolhouse.

This chapter revisits the Framework for School Culture and their Unifying Elements highlighting critical insights and major ideas throughout the book about how culture is foundational to the work of teachers and leaders to improve the learning experiences for their students. Major takeaways are offered to help leaders and teachers to reflect about the work needed to support a positive school culture.

 # Revisiting the Framework for School Culture

In Chapter 1, the Framework for School Culture was presented in Figure 1.1 in the form of an iceberg that serves to anchor teacher voice and agency as the foundation needed to build collective responsibility within the school. Referring to Figure 1.1, the visual image shows the tip of the iceberg. School climate is at the tip, its most visible point. It is here at the tip where everyone can see the behaviors and their impact. These behaviors include, for example, genuine collaboration between teachers and leaders, working on common goals within the context of the school and its classrooms.

At the center of the iceberg is school culture. Notice that the spiral pushes up to the tip of the iceberg. In other words, the culture of a school greatly influences what happens outwardly visible at the tip, school climate.

Next in the iceberg comes a waterline. Residing immediately below the waterline are the *Unifying Elements*. These unifying elements include a sense of belonging, professional engagement, empowerment, self-efficacy, and others. The attention paid to nurturing these unifying elements determine whether a culture is positive or toxic. The arrows across and between the unifying elements represent that these elements are

- dynamic illustrating that there is interplay between them;
- embedded and deeply rooted under the hood of the culture;
- not hierarchical or linear; ordering occurs above, below, and/or at the same level with each other; and,
- what reinforces teacher voice and teacher agency.

The unifying elements, when examined in their totality, are the culture.

The Framework for School Culture suggests that school leaders and teachers must *intentionally look below the surface* of the waterline to see how all the unifying elements can be nurtured to improve a school's culture. The work supporting a positive school culture is messy and recursive. The work follows many ebbs and flows as schools address the complexities of working with students, teachers, parents, and others who are a part of the school and its community. The unifying elements in the Framework for School Culture can help define and make sense of school culture.

Unifying Elements of School Culture

Regardless if the culture is positive or toxic, teachers are the culture leaders of the school. School culture is greatly influenced by their voice and agency. Teacher voice and agency are the cultural anchors and provide the fuel needed to create the synergy for the movement within the unifying elements. Voice occurs when teachers share thoughts and ideas in an environment of mutual trust and respect. Agency occurs when teachers are empowered to act on their knowledge of children and their beliefs that the work they are doing is important. It is only through the individual and collective voices of teachers that they will be able to act purposely and constructively.

Throughout the chapters in this book, the unifying elements that shape, support, and influence culture have been examined. A few ideas to keep in mind are offered:

- The unifying elements do not unfold in a black box.
- There is a synergy between the unifying elements. That is, the unifying elements are influenced by the presence or the absence of one another.
- School culture is shaped by the interaction and coherence between the unifying elements.

A positive school culture can only be realized when leaders understand the impact of the relationship between the unifying elements. The unifying elements must not be viewed as independent parts but as dynamic and ever flowing entities. Although relational to each other, each unifying element has its own unique characteristics. As a refresher, the unifying elements are recapped.

Empowerment

Empowering teachers requires leaders to share authority over decisions in the classroom and to promote teacher input and decision-making authority in larger issues such as school-wide policies and procedures. When leaders empower teachers, they create a culture that supports the development of competence. When leaders promote empowerment, they invest in building human capital, supporting the growth of individual teachers and the teams they serve on and the committees in which they participate.

Autonomy

When teachers are empowered, they have the autonomy to make critical decisions that are paramount to their abilities to meet the diverse learning needs of their students. Teachers must have the freedom to make pivots in their classrooms based on their students' needs and interests. Teachers cannot be limited to one size fits all prescriptive lessons. Furthermore, autonomy grants teachers the flexibility in their decisions to grow personally and professionally by having the freedom to personalize their own professional learning (see Chapters 1 and 2).

Collaboration

Collaboration is a powerful unifying element within a school's culture. Collaboration occurs both formally through clearly identified structures such as common planning time and informally through conversations that teachers have in the hallways, the parking lot, and other such places that teachers meet. Collaboration allows teachers to grow professionally by sharing effective practices with one another, engaging in thought provoking discussions, and reflecting about their experiences (see Chapter 5). It is through collaboration that relationships are built, practices are shared, and teachers engage in conversations about how to improve their instructional practices.

Support, Care, and Safety

Support, care, and safety are vital to the school house. Teachers have a vital need of care and to feel safe both physically and emotionally. A culture of care is created when leaders serve as role models of care, engage in personal and professional conversations, provide opportunities for others to practice care and their ability to bring out the best in teachers. Teachers also need to feel safe. Safety and security are basic needs in Maslow's Hierarchy of Basic Needs. Teachers need and want to feel that they are safe and supported by their school leaders as well as their teaching colleagues (see Chapters 4 and 5).

Sense of Belonging

Everyone wants to feel that they belong, that they are valued, and that they are a member of a community. A sense of belonging counters the isolation teachers often experience when they spend hours in the day with sparse contact with their colleagues. A culture with a strong sense of belonging built through relationships helps teachers bring meaning to their work, increases their engagement in the profession, supports professional growth, and increases their sense of efficacy.

It is important for teachers to derive meaning from their work, increase their commitment, feel part of the community, and grow professionally. Cultures with a strong sense of belonging are strengthened through teacher conversations, and help to motivate teachers even during the most challenging and stressful times (see Chapters 4 and 5).

Self and Collective Efficacy

Self and Collective Efficacy are now increasingly critical factors in school culture as teacher's question their confidence in their abilities to be successful. Self and collective efficacy are developed when individual teachers and the larger collective of teachers believe they have the ability to create meaningful change. Teachers are more open and willing to be innovative in their practices, shoulder school turbulence, and are more supportive of students when they believe they can make a difference (see Chapters 1 and 3).

Professional Engagement

Professional Engagement is needed to harness the knowledge and experience teachers hold that is necessary to improve schools (see Chapter 1). Leaders have a responsibility to create a work environment that is resilient in the midst of change and where teachers are engaged and feel valued as an integral part of the schools (see Chapter 2). Furthermore, teacher engagement is the foundation to creating change by providing opportunities for them to challenge assumptions and see a different world view of the work needed to support students and each other (see Chapter 3).

Creating opportunities for teachers to engage with one another also requires leaders to intentionally redirect efforts to support teachers as they embark on the complexities of their work. Critical for leaders is creating structures for them to have ongoing conversation about their practice and relevant professional learning (see Chapter 5).

Teacher Voice and Teacher Agency

Teacher voice and agency are the cultural anchors required to create the synergy for the continuous interactions and changes between the unifying elements. Through teacher voice and agency, new opportunities are created for improving schools differently from past practices predicated on top-down leadership approaches (see Chapter 1). School culture is systematically changed when leaders recognize the positive impact when teachers have a voice and can take actions to improve their schools. A school culture supports improvement efforts and buffers internal and external disruptions when its teachers have the ability to own and act on their beliefs, knowledge, and expertise they bring to the school (see Chapter 7). This work cannot wait for tomorrow or when things settle down. The time is now.

Asking, Why Culture Now

While schools have always experienced shifts in their culture resulting from internal and external factors, the current conditions in which schools operate is placing them in a perilous position. The impact of COVID-19 when the school doors closed and the resulting political rifts alone have engulfed schools. The life internal to the school as we know it has been thrown into whirlwinds of change in areas spanning from teacher work conditions, engagement, and teacher retention and attrition.

Externally, the escalating pressures from increased teacher shortages, poverty, changing demographics, and student mobility continue to test how schools' function and the impact of each on school culture. While schools have always been centered in political positioning, a new and fast-growing divided nation politically is creating new pressures from not only politicians, but also from within schools, school boards, parents, students, teachers, and leaders.

Amid these internal and external pressures, there is one certainty for success: success rises and falls on the school culture. School culture is foundational in how schools function. Culture can be both the buffer during internal and external turbulence as well as the catalyst to leverage positive change and innovation.

Culture has and will continue to be foundational to the totality of work required for schools to fulfill their responsibilities. In today's environment, the role of culture has emerged as the most significant asset to schools in the midst of turbulence. The success of schools moving forward will require leaders to leverage the power of culture by assuming an active role in examining how it is influenced by the unifying elements in the Framework for School Culture (see Chapter 1).

Too often, leveraging the power of culture is not a school improvement strategy used by leaders because typically, leaders develop strategies that are more tangible in design and implementation (see Chapter 3). However, school culture, when understood and defined, is a unique and untapped resource when connected to school improvement efforts (see Chapter 1). Shafer (2018) reminds us that culture is "not as a hazy mass of intangibles" (para 4) and that principals must begin to envision how culture plays a significant role in school improvement efforts.

Developing a supportive teaching and learning culture for improvement is strategic. It requires leaders to shape school culture by understanding the elements of its composition as described and outlined in the unifying elements in the Framework for School Culture. The work needed to support a culture for teaching and learning begins with those who have the greatest impact on learning—Teachers. Teachers are schools' largest assets, and they have critical insights both individually and collectively on how their school's culture supports their work. Culture evolves from not just the voices of teachers, but also through their agency to innovate in schools where workplace conditions support collaborative practices in which solutions can be generated. Supportive school cultures are created when teachers are valued and when they know they are having an impact in the daily lives of their students. For teachers, it is all about a culture that supports them in doing their best work.

Culture may look different from the inside-out as compared to the outside-in, especially when it is not defined. Too often, comments about culture are made as one walks through the schoolhouse door "this is a great school culture." Is it? School culture may look and feel different when you look beyond the entrance of the school building. For leaders, school culture goes beyond the schoolhouse door and requires them to understand the unifying elements identified in the school culture framework (Chapter 1) and enact the processes to create synergy with these unifying elements through teacher voice and agency.

The role of the leader is to support and foster a continuous process of improvement that is pivotal in developing a positive school culture. This role encompasses how leaders understand the dynamics of their schools' culture and how they embrace the human side of developing relationships, fostering a sense of belonging, empowering teachers, addressing the tensions associated with autonomy. All against the backdrop of promoting self- and collective-efficacy, while simultaneously supporting the structures that enable teachers and leaders to work collectively to do their very best work with students—and each other. A positive school culture supports teachers.

Culture Supports Teachers

Teacher support is demonstrated in many ways but none more important than developing a culture where teachers are valued, and they have professional opportunities to lead curricular, instructional, and professional development efforts while collaborating on the formulation of school policies and procedures. Leaders have a responsibility to create the workplace conditions with attention to the barriers and supports that teachers need to grow as professionals (see Chapters 1 and 5). The will of teachers to succeed with their students is high. However, the internal and external factors that impact this will must be supported by the culture in which they work, especially given the increasingly challenging situations they currently face.

With a focus on leading culture by developing strong relationships and understanding the emerging needs of teachers, leaders better position themselves by supporting what is most important, which ultimately is the work of teachers in the classroom. Strong relationships emerge from critical culture norms including collegiality, trust, appreciation and recognition, open and honest communication, and involvement in decision making (see Chapter 3). Furthermore, supporting teachers through a cultural lens recognizes the power of human capital and creates the conditions needed for individual teachers and the relationships between teachers as a collective to have the greatest impact on their work (see Chapter 7).

When leaders understand the relationships between the unifying elements, they can develop powerful school cultures through their relationships and actions, the ways they communicate, and the respect and honesty they exhibit when interacting with teachers (see Chapter 4). When teachers work in a culture of trust and supportive working conditions, they are more effective, stay in their schools, grow professionally, and collectively engage in improvement.

Teacher Effectiveness

Teacher effectiveness can no longer improve in isolation and no longer can teacher effectiveness be measured solely by test scores. Teacher effectiveness stems from a culture where everyone is focused on improving student learning using multiple metrics while at the same time modeling improvements in their own practices. Teacher effectiveness improves when teachers work in cultures of trust. Furthermore, cultures that support effective teacher conversations on practice, innovation, and risk taking create a needed sense of pride, creativity, and ownership (see Chapters 3 and 6).

Teacher Retention

Teacher retention continues to be a growing concern exacerbated by the decreased number of post-secondary students entering the teaching profession. Teachers thrive in cultures where they collaborate, are valued and respected, and trusted to make good instructional decisions in the classroom (see Chapter 2). School leaders must identify strengths and needs as they seek to retain teachers and support them. Schools with positive cultures of affiliation and belonging support retention, reduce isolation, and speak to the ethos of care and concern for each other (see Chapter 5).

Professional Learning

Professional learning and agency are essential as teachers seek to improve their instructional expertise. Teachers want to learn and to grow as they move throughout their careers. Leaders need to be attuned to the professional needs of teachers and to create a culture to support teachers as they embark on the complexities of teaching. Teachers need and want to engage in professional job-embedded learning supported through conversations and practices that nurture growth (Zepeda, 2019). Professional Learning Communities (PLCs) is an example of one construct that allows teachers to interact with each other to improve their effectiveness by accessing teacher expertise and experiences, engaging in purposeful professional learning, and providing safety nets for innovation (see Chapters 1, 3, and 4).

Workplace Conditions

Workplace conditions must support teaching and learning. However, not all schools have the same working conditions. Leaders should keep in mind that teachers from different backgrounds might be affected differently by their working conditions. A primary responsibility of school and district leaders is to understand the unique characteristics of their culture and the diverse needs of their faculty in creating the working conditions needed especially in times of rapid change. Moreover, the workplace conditions today need to include physical and social emotional support for teachers in the system (see Chapters 2 and 4).

Collective Responsibility and Ownership

Collective responsibility and ownership begin with leaders sending messages that the collective work of all teachers is what will make a difference for students (see Chapter 5). A culture of collective responsibility and ownership reflects a belief that all students can achieve, supports individual teachers especially those new to the teaching profession, creates opportunities for teachers to share effective practices, and systematically have opportunities to learn together through team based professional learning.

Developing a culture of collective responsibility also requires leaders to promote teacher leaders by providing opportunities for them to engage with each other about professional practice, support innovation and risk taking, and provide feedback to support the growth and development of leadership skills (see Chapter 6).

Human and Social Capital

School cultures where leaders value supporting teachers build needed human and social capital within their system. Human capital recognizes the value that each person brings to the organization and how the school benefits from having the person work there. Equally important is social capital that promotes the sharing of ideas and information between teachers and leaders. Social capital recognizes the talents of teachers and highlights the importance of the interactions between peers. Positive school cultures that have the greatest impact on students are ones that support and value the expertise of teachers individually and collectively (see Chapter 6).

Key takeaways from this book can support leaders and teachers to understand and embrace the influences that culture has on their work.

 # Key Takeaways About School Culture

School culture is complex in its nature and definition. However, school culture can no longer be an afterthought to improving schools. School culture is foundational to navigating the changing internal and external dynamics that influence schools every day. However, developing a positive and supportive school culture is not the result of random acts or relying on historical trajectories that are predictable. Developing a positive school culture requires definition, strategic planning, and collective action by leaders and teachers.

At the center of school culture are the connections and relationships between the unifying elements described throughout this book and their relationships to each other. Teachers are able to do their best work when school leaders understand the dynamics of culture and are able to lead with a culture lens. For teachers to do their best work, they need a school culture that is supportive and allows them to professionally grow to meet the changing dynamics of teaching and learning. School culture is dynamic and not static, and is influenced daily and overtime by the collective actions of teachers and leaders in the system.

The following takeaways from the book reflect key points in leading through a culture lens, the value of culture in improving teaching and learning, and how culture is influenced collectively.

Leading Through a School Culture Lens

- Leaders who establish and maintain high levels of trust understand how their personal and professional behaviors positively or negatively contribute to the norms within their school culture.

- Leaders must be able to identify and articulate the dynamics between school culture and climate and how such dynamics are both overlapping yet distinctly unique.

- Teacher leaders influence their colleagues to improve educational practice and accept collective responsibility for improved outcomes.

- Collaborative cultures are created when leaders engage, support, and empower teachers to make instructional decisions.

- Leaders must identify and be responsive to the subcultures that exist within the broader school culture in the building.

Promoting a Culture for Teaching and Learning

- Teacher ownership for school culture and improvement occurs through specific, sustained practices that encourage agency and engagement.

- School culture is influenced by leveraging the power of teacher voice and agency.

- Teacher collaboration is defined as ways in which they work together to improve student outcomes, refine classroom practices, and create opportunities for job-embedded professional learning.

- A school culture built through teacher professional learning communities, which may include collaborative teacher teams, online communities, mentorships, and teacher induction programs is critically important in redefining how teachers interact with one another.

- Peer coaching, teacher reflection, and extended conversations are essential to teacher collaborative practices.

Situating School Culture at the Center of the Collective Work

- The internal dynamics—defined by the actions, beliefs, voice, and agency of teachers and principals—will shape school culture and impact student achievement.

- Coherence is achieved when strategies and processes are aligned to the content and purposes of professional learning.

- Collective responsibility is developed when teachers and leaders lead together focusing on gains in student achievement.

- Turbulence, regardless of whether the disruption originates inside or outside of the school building, may have personal and professional impact on staff.

- School culture will evolve, especially during times of cultural turbulence; therefore, leaders must be intentional about clarifying for teachers what is and is not going to change.

School reform efforts to improve teaching and learning will come and go, but a school's culture will always be ever present. Research and case studies have consistently reported that a positive school culture is a mainstay for teachers to be effective; yet, their voices and actions to improve culture have too often taken a minimal role in school improvement efforts.

It is a new and different day in education. Knowing teachers have the greatest impact on a students' achievement leaves no options in improvement efforts other than to focus on how to support them, which is through culture. We must understand how a school culture is shaped through the voice and actions of teachers and how culture influences their work. Why? Because "it is all about culture."

References

Shafer, L. (2018). *What makes a good school culture?* Harvard Graduate School of Education. www.gse.harvard.edu/news/uk/18/07/what-makes-good-school-culture

Zepeda, S. J. (2019). *Professional development: What works* (3rd ed.). Routledge.

Index

Note: Page numbers in *italics* indicate figures, and page numbers in **bold** indicate tables on the corresponding pages.